Outpourings Of A Beloved Heart

A 30 day poetry devotional about God's love

Joan Embola

Outpourings Of A Beloved Heart

A 30 day poetry devotional about God's love

Copyright © 2018 by Joan N. Embola

All rights reserved.

ISBN: 1976131650

ISBN-13: 978-1976131653

Dedication

I dedicate this book to my Heavenly Father- the Almighty God who made this project possible. I would never have gotten this far without Him.

I also dedicate it to my mum, dad and brothers for being an excellent support system to me. I am truly blessed to have you all in my life.

And to all the other special people in my life who believed in me and encouraged me to keep going when doubts came, I am very grateful. Thank you for all your input. You know yourselves.

I love you all.

Table of Contents

Author's Testimony 1

Part One: Our Loving Creator 5

   A Love Better Than Life 6

   My Great God 12

   You Know It All 18

   You Are Bigger 24

   Master Of The Waves 29

   Every Morning 35

   Changes 40

Part Two: Our Disobedient Hearts 46

   Your Love Don't Care 47

   Rescue Me Lord 53

Part Three: Our Rescue 61

   Blessed Baby Jesus 62

   The One My Heart Loves 67

   Your Grace 74

   In Your Presence 79

Part Four: Our Identity 85

   Not Good Enough? 86

Part Five: Our Purpose 94

   I Bow My Head In Worship 95

   I Give You All Of Me 101

   The Way Of Life 107

Doubts 113

Part Six: Our Comfort 120

I Wonder Why 121

Near To My Broken Heart 127

You Kept Me 134

Trusting You 139

My Hope 144

I Will Wait On You 149

To The One Who Holds My Tomorrow 154

Give Me Faith 159

If Not, You Are Still Good 165

Part Seven: Our Future Glory 172

This Too Shall Pass 173

Streets Of Gold 178

Blessed Be Your Holy Name 184

Author's Testimony

Outpourings Of A Beloved Heart

Dear beloved one,

Before you jump straight into this book, I'd like to tell you a little bit about the inspiration behind it and I hope you don't mind.

Over the past few years, God has taken me on a journey to discover my true identity and He has brought me through so many situations that have made me discover who I am as **His beloved one.** I grew up in a Christian home so the whole concept of God and Christianity has never been strange to me. However, it took me a while to discover that Christianity is not just a religion but a relationship between the Creator and His beloved ones.

Since the day Jesus changed my heart, I have come to know and understand what true joy, comfort and peace feel like- even in the midst of storms. Most importantly, I have been able to experience true love in Christ and this is a priceless treasure which the world will never be able to substitute.

This journey of mine has been a roller coaster ride filled with tears, hurt, laughter, brokenness, healing, mountains and valleys. But through it all, God has been faithful and He has taught me to trust His love.

"So we have come to know and to believe the love that God has for us. God is love and whoever abides in love, abides in God, and God abides in Him"

-1 John 4:16

One thing that God has shown me in this journey is that He has given each and every one of us gifts which we can use to glorify Him. I guess I could say that writing is one of those gifts for me. I have been journaling for about 4 years now and I have also been writing poems since I was 13 years old. I never had any intentions of sharing these poems with anyone but recently, God has shown me that He has the power to use my work for His glory.

So here I am, overcoming my fear of criticism and self-doubt and sharing with you some of the poems I have written over the years. My heart has found true love in Christ and it is overflowing with so many testimonies.

I can't keep these testimonies to myself so I decided to tell them through the poetry and reflections you will find in this book. All the poems were inspired by personal experiences in

Outpourings Of A Beloved Heart

my life and they tell a story of how God's love has sustained me through it all. The words you will find in this book are the outpourings of a heart that has found true solace in the arms of a loving God.

I implore you to please pray before you read each entry and ask the Holy Spirit to open your eyes so you can see the message He has for you through these words. Take these truths about God's loving promises and meditate on them. Apply them to your life and to whatever situation you are going through. Prophesy His love into your life until your heart believes the truth that you are **His beloved one,** deeply treasured and dearly loved by Him.

I pray that this book will encourage you to spend more time in God's presence so you will get to know Him for yourself. I pray that it will inspire you to go deeper into your relationship with Him so you will be able to stand confidently on the truths portrayed in His Word. I also pray that it will encourage you to see that God's sovereign love towards you always prevails come what may. Hope you are encouraged. God bless you.

Joanny 🤍

PART ONE:

OUR LOVING CREATOR

"The Lord is gracious and compassionate, slow to anger and rich in love. The Lord is good to all; He has compassion on all He has made."

Psalm 145:8-9

Day 1: A Love Better Than Life

Outpourings Of A Beloved Heart

So pure

So unchanging

So precious

So fulfilling, it always leaves me wanting more

So timeless

So steadfast

So unconditional

So refreshing, it infuses my soul from the crown of my head to the soles of my feet

Your love oh Lord

Yes, Your love

Your love took me away from the rejection of men

It picked me up and restored my faith in You

Your love met me bound to the chains of sin

It freed me and gave me a new song to sing

Your love met me broken and in the dark

It became a lamp for my feet and a light to my path

Outpourings Of A Beloved Heart

Your love filled my heart with reasons to rejoice

And it guided me back into Your presence

The more I live in Your presence Lord,

The more You capture my heart

And the more I fall in love with You

For no one can handle my heart as gently as You do

Your love is so gracious

So kind

So merciful

Yes, Your love

It is so captivating

So flawless

So empowering

Yes, Your love

I need it every hour of every day

I need it forever and always

For Your love is better than life

Reflections

Scripture: Psalm 63:1-5

God's love is all around us and this truth still stands even in the world we live in today. Many heart breaking events happening in our world seem to point us towards everything that would be the opposite of love. And it may even be fair to say that our world is broken because all we need to do now is look at the news headlines to see evidence that hatred, anger and division have taken over.

But in spite of all these things, there is one truth that still remains. God's love is all around us. **Psalm 63** was written by King David while he was in the desert of Judah. He was in this dry and weary land with no water yet, he still expressed his longing and desperation for God's love.

The psalmist proclaimed that he had beheld God's power and glory and that the only thing capable of bringing him satisfaction in that desert was God's love. He then went on to say that he longed for God's love because it is better than life itself (**Verse 3**). This declaration came from a man who had fully experienced the fullness of the love of God.

The Bible teaches that it was because of God's love for us that He created us and breathed the breath of life into our lungs so that we could become living beings (**Genesis 2:7**). It is because of His love for us that we are able to live, move and even exist (**Acts 17:28**). Each breath we take is a testament to His love and He is our life support.

Do the troubles in our world today make it seem like you too are in a dry, parched and weary land just like King David was? In this desert place, what are you longing for? Are you longing for God's love too? Are you longing for His presence and to see the fullness of His glory? Does your soul always hunger and thirst for Him? Are you sensitive to His love? Do you truly believe that His love is better than life itself?

It would be interesting to know what inspired King David to make such a powerful declaration and as you go through this book, my prayer is that you too will become more sensitive to God's love and that His presence will be all you seek. I also pray that hopefully, you will be able to declare in your heart and believe without any doubts that His love for you is better than life itself.

As you step out today, you can take comfort in His love for you. Seek His loving face always, spend time in His presence and let Him fill your heart with the joy and peace that flows freely from His throne. He loves you.

Prayer: *Heavenly Father, thank You for Your love which gives me life. Please help me to be more sensitive to it today. Help me to take comfort in it even in this broken world. In Jesus' name. Amen.*

Today's affirmation: *I will seek God's love always because it is better than life.*

Day 2: My Great God

Outpourings Of A Beloved Heart

The greatness of my God I cannot comprehend

My human mind cannot fathom His majesty

My soul can do nothing but bow down

I bow down in worship of my great God

He is the ancient of days and in the beginning,

He spoke the earth and the heavens into form

He has a name above all and at the mention of His name,

The earth trembles at His feet

He is El, Eloah- mighty and strong

He parted the Red Sea and His children walked through unharmed

He is Elohim- Creator of the universe

And He is also the Creator of my heart

He is Adonai- Lord over all

He reigns supreme in the heavens and the earth is His footstool

He is Jehovah Jireh- my provider

For He can make a way where there is none

Outpourings Of A Beloved Heart

He is Jehovah Rapha- the great physician

He is the Sun of righteousness with healing in His wings

He is Jehovah Nissi- the mighty man in battle

He is my rallying place, my safety and my rock

He is Jehovah M'kaddesh- holy and pure

He is glorious in holiness and awesome in splendour

He is Jehovah Shalom- my peace

His peace transcends all human understanding

He is Jehovah Tsidkenu- my very source of righteousness

He is upright and without injustice

He is Jehovah Raah- my shepherd

He is God and He never leads me wrong

He is Jehovah Shammah- the "I AM"

For He was, He is and He always will be

He is El Roi- the One who sees and knows me

He knows my deepest thoughts and He loves me still

He is El- Olam- the beginning and the end

Outpourings Of A Beloved Heart

My God is timeless

He is never failing

His name is Yahweh

The greatness of my God I cannot comprehend

For my human mind cannot fathom such a love so deep

The love only shown by my God

My great God

Reflections:

Scripture: 1 Chronicles 29:10-13

Taking a good look around our world again, we would notice the chirping birds on the trees and the beautiful flowers growing by the sidewalk which we can often overlook. The vast seas and tall mountains are also not excluded from this masterpiece which was put together by The Great Artist- our Heavenly Father.

These things which our eyes see are more than just seas, mountains, birds or flowers. They are all different ways in which the greatness of our Creator is being portrayed (**Romans 1:20**). Our Heavenly Father so perfectly designed the heavens and the earth without any mistakes and He also created us- His children, in His image and we are part of this masterpiece (**Genesis 1:26**).

Outpourings Of A Beloved Heart

God is not only great because of what He has created or what He has done. He is great because He is God. Period. The Bible reminds us that He reigns supreme in the heavens and that He is headship and Lord over all. He is so mighty and strong that no one can stop His hand **(Isaiah 14:27).**

But what is comforting about God's love is that even in His supremacy, mighty power and all His splendour, He still thinks about us (**Psalm 136:23**). He made this great world of ours and He looks after His creation day and night (**Psalm 121:3-4**) and even the chirping birds flying over our heads and the flowers in the fields do not have to worry because He looks after them too. We are constantly on His mind and He never forgets about us (**Psalm 115:12**).

Do you find it hard to entertain the fact that the same Creator of the universe loves you too? While it may be hard to believe that such a big God is mindful of you, it is the truth so the next time you catch a sunset or a sunrise and stand in awe of its beauty, think also about the One who created the sun. Take comfort in this truth today; **the hand of God that instructs the sun to rise and set every day is the same hand that lifts your head high**. He loves you.

Prayer: *Heavenly Father, thank You for Your great and mighty power which You reveal to me every day. Thank You for being who You are as God. Help me today not to forget the comforting reassurance that I was created by Your mighty hand and that I am always on Your mind. In Jesus' name. Amen.*

Today's affirmation: *The Most High God cares about me. He is thinking about me right now.*

Day 3: You Know It All

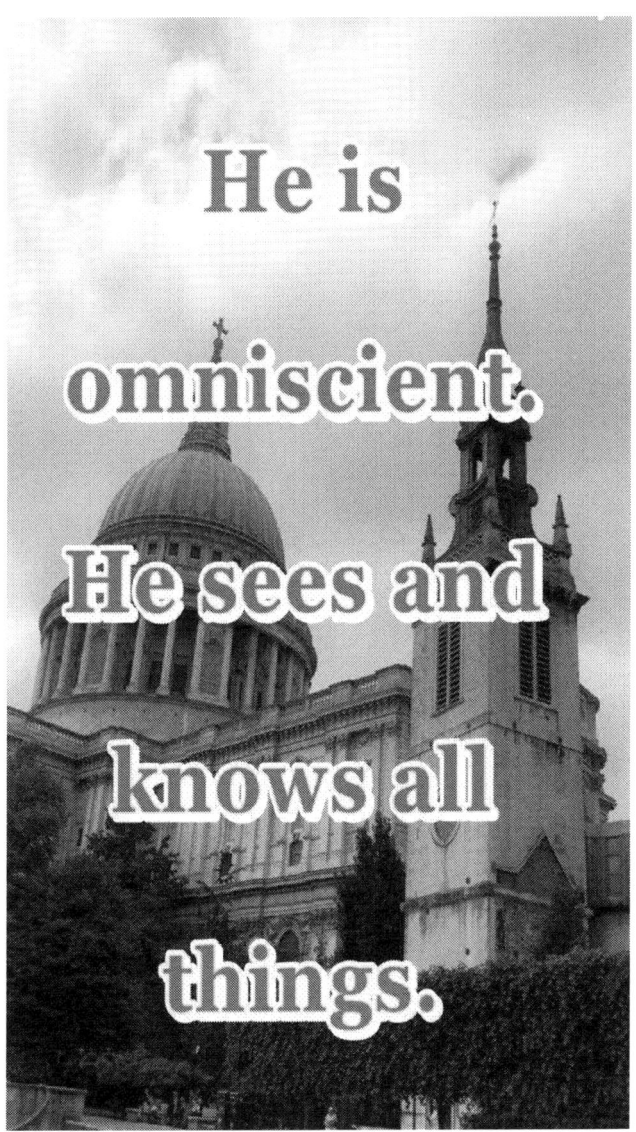

Outpourings Of A Beloved Heart

You knew me in my mother's womb

Before I was brought forth into this world to bloom

You know the day I was born

When I let out cries like a horn

You knew me as a child when I tried to flourish in this world

You knew all my daily struggles- hair in braids or plaits, straight or curled

You knew all the fears that made me cry

And in those moments You stood as my rock so high

You know when I wake up and when I sleep

Because indeed You neither slumber nor sleep

You know when I come in and when I go out

And You are there to protect me without a doubt

You know all what I've been through

How hard it is sometimes when I don't have a clue

You know my strengths and when I am weak

But even in my weakness, Your comfort is at its peak

Outpourings Of A Beloved Heart

You know my joys and You know the pain I feel

You know how the tears roll down and stain my cheeks

You know when I fall and when I hide from You

Yet Your love pursues me and always pulls me through

You know the little things that keep me awake at night

And Your loving arms are always around me so tight

You know my worries, the trials and temptations I face

And You let me seek strength in Your loving face

You know when my heart gets broken

You know where to find the pieces and put it together as one

For You made this heart of mine

And You know how to love it with all Your might

You know me Lord more than I know myself

And You know how to draw this heart of mine to thyself

I know You care and know all about me

And so I have confidence that You will take care of me

Reflections

Scripture: Psalm 139:1-16

A friend of mine once tried to tell me about a situation he was going through and when he explained to me how he was feeling, I couldn't fully understand where he was coming from. In the end, he gave up trying to explain and said "Never mind. I'll take it to God."

This made me realise an important aspect of God's love. He is omniscient. He knows all things, sees all things and He understands all things. Even though my friend found it hard to explain exactly how he felt, he knew our Heavenly Father was definitely going to understand. Wouldn't it be such a shame if there was absolutely no one who could understand exactly how we are feeling?

Jesus Christ was God in human form and while He was here on earth, He lived just like us and felt pain like us. He wept when His friend- Lazarus died (**John 11:35**) and He also suffered the pain of being betrayed by one of His disciples (**Luke 22:4-6**).

When He was arrested and needed support, almost all of those who were close to Him deserted Him (**Mark 14:50**). He was killed by the very ones He loved and those He had come to save. He knows what it feels like to be in a desolate place and He knows about how we feel too.

The Bible teaches that God knows what we think and He knows what we want to say before we even say it **(Psalm 139:4).** Whether we ride the wings of the morning or dwell by the farthest oceans, He knows. He knows every single detail of our lives and He wants us to bring them to Him in prayer.

You know that time you felt hurt and betrayed? He knows about it.

That unpleasant feeling you can't explain? He knows about it.

That exam you feel really anxious about? Yes, He knows about that too.

Those debts and bills you are struggling to pay? He knows about them.

Even those worries that give you sleepless nights? Guess who knows about them? That's right. God knows all about them.

As you go through the day, take all your worries to Him in prayer. Even the things you believe to be insignificant, He wants to hear about those too. **Take them to Him in prayer so He can give you peace and comfort**. He cares about you. He understands and He loves you.

Prayer: *Heavenly Father, thank You so much for the confident assurance I have that You know me more than I know myself. Please help me to trust Your love today and to lay all my cares and worries at Your feet because You understand and You will take care of me. In Jesus' name. Amen*

Today's affirmation: *God knows my name and He knows my story. He will take care of me.*

Day 4: You Are Bigger

Outpourings Of A Beloved Heart

You are bigger than the fears that try to stifle me

You are bigger than the challenges that try to hinder me

You are bigger than the obstacles that try to overpower me

You are bigger than everything

You are bigger than the sorrows that try to break me

You are bigger than the pain that tries to crush me

You are bigger than the mountains that try to stop me

You are bigger than everything

You are bigger than all my pain and loss

You are bigger than my sins for which You were nailed on the cross

You are bigger than death which You conquered like a boss

You are bigger than everything

You are bigger than all my debts which You so willingly paid

You are even bigger than the devil who comes to betray

That's why I can always confidently say

You are bigger than everything

Reflections

Scripture: Numbers 13:21-33

When God delivered the Israelites out of Egypt, He promised to lead them into a land flowing with milk and honey. However, when they got to this land, they found that other people were already living in it and this was an obstacle for them.

At God's command, Moses sent spies to go and check out the land and most of them came back with a report that instilled fear in the people. The spies saw the giants living in the land and they were terrified. They believed that the Israelites would seem like grasshoppers going against these giants (**Numbers 13:33**) and they didn't think the Israelites stood a chance.

The people had forgotten that God was the One who delivered them out of slavery in Egypt (**Exodus 6:6**). They had forgotten that He split the Red Sea so they could walk through on dry land (**Exodus 14:21**) and He saved them from the hands of the Egyptians who wanted to kill them. They had also forgotten that this same God was still on their side.

Perhaps you too are in a devastating situation right now. Perhaps you see your troubles like giants and yourself like a grasshopper standing before them. Perhaps you are just as terrified as the spies were and you feel you are not strong enough to fight. Remember this today; **you do not have to be a giant because God has got you in the hollow of His hands and He will do the fighting for you**.

Instead of allowing fear overpower you, step up boldly with the confidence you have in Christ just like Caleb did and tell these supposed giants in your life how big your God is. You are safe whatever comes your way. God is bigger than those troubles you face and His power and might always prevail. He will fight for you because He loves you.

Prayer: *Heavenly Father, thank You for Your amazing power which keeps me safe whatever comes my way. Please help me today to trust that You are bigger than all my troubles. In Jesus' name. Amen.*

Today's Affirmation: *God is bigger than all my troubles. He will fight for me.*

Day 5: Master Of The Waves

Outpourings Of A Beloved Heart

"Thum thum thum"

The waves of life hit my boat

Just like a beating drum

My enemies look at me and gloat

"Where is Your God?", they ask

"Why can't He save You now?"

"Is your God asleep?", they ask

"Why can't He save You now?"

So in my misery, I cry out

Why are You so silent?

These waves are going to knock me out

How can You be so silent?

Then, in the midst of the storm, You come

For You are the Master of the waves

You are Jehovah Shalom

And You are the Might One who saves

And so You ask me, "Why do you not trust?"

Outpourings Of A Beloved Heart

"O ye of little faith?"

"I raised you up from the dust"

"And I can calm the waves with your faith"

"Peace, be still", You say to the waves

For they know You and obey Your voice

By Your word alone You calm the waves

And You take away all the noise

So, to my enemies who used to gloat

Those who thought I could not be saved

My Lord has stilled my rocking boat

And He remains the Master of the waves

Reflections

Scripture: Mark 4:35-41

Jesus and His disciples were encountered by a storm when they were crossing the lake to the other side and Jesus was sleeping peacefully through it. The Bible describes this storm as vicious and the disciples were overwhelmed with fear. They thought they were going to drown and in their despair, they cried out to Jesus.

Outpourings Of A Beloved Heart

In the midst of that storm, the disciples wondered why Jesus was sleeping and if He even cared about them. They wondered if Jesus was going to let them die. "Master, do you not care if we drown?" they cried out. And even though they had seen Jesus perform a number of miracles before, this storm pushed them to question His loyalty.

When the storms of life rock our boat from side to side, it may sometimes feel like God is sleeping and that He can't see our situation. In these trying times, how we choose to respond is very important. It is easy to be overwhelmed with fear just like the disciples were and sometimes we just want to cuss and get angry at God. But please don't.

It may be easier to break down and give up than to hold on. It may also be easier to just let the storm take over but instead of complaining and questioning, we need to cry out to the Master of the waves- Jesus Christ.

There was absolutely no need for the disciples to have been afraid. If only they knew they had the Master of the waves in that boat with them, they would have been sleeping too just like Jesus was because **in Christ, we find rest, even in the midst of the storm.**

We see that when Jesus calmed the storm, the disciples were so amazed that they exclaimed "What kind of man is this? Even the winds and waves obey Him!" Do you know the kind of God you serve? Do you know that He is able to do exceedingly, abundantly above all that you could ever ask or think?

The winds and waves know His voice and they will always bow down to Him. He will step in at the perfect time to deliver you and even as you wait, He will give you peace as

Outpourings Of A Beloved Heart

He leads you through it all. So if the storms of life rock your boat today, cry out to the Master of the waves. He will give you peace so You can rest in Him. He will give you peace because He loves you.

Prayer: *Heavenly Father, thank You because You hear me when I cry out to You. Thank You because even in the midst of the storm, You are with me. Please calm my worrying heart today and give me rest when the storms of life rock my boat. In Jesus' name. Amen.*

Today's affirmation: *God is the Master of the waves and He will give me peace.*

Day 6: Every Morning

Outpourings Of A Beloved Heart

Every morning, Your grace is new

It forgets that I was a wretch undeserving of You

And that I was blind, lost and far from You

As fresh as the morning dew,

Your grace for me is always new

Every morning, Your mercies are new

They forget about my sins of yesterday

The sins that led me astray

As fresh as the sunrise each day,

Your mercies towards me are always new

Every morning, Your love is new

It forgets that I despised You yesterday

And that my heart had turned from Your ways

But as fresh as the hope is for a new day,

Your love for me is always new

Reflections

Scripture: Lamentations 3:22-23

The lyrics to one of my favourite worship songs were taken from **Lamentations 3:22-23** and it says,

> **"The steadfast love of the Lord never ceases.**
>
> **His mercies never come to an end.**
>
> **They are new every morning.**
>
> **Great is thy faithfulness"**

For many years, I had been singing this song over and over again but I had never really taken time out to think about what the lyrics meant. One clear truth that stands out in these verses is the fact that God's love for us is renewed every single day.

The word **"renew"** means to give fresh life to something, to strengthen, to revive and to restore. It also means to rejuvenate, to resuscitate and to awaken. One definition I particularly loved after doing a quick online search was **"to bring back to an original condition of freshness and vigour"**.

God's love for you is always as fresh as ever. **His love never runs out no matter what you do, what you say or where you go.** How amazing is that? Please take some time to think about it. Imagine buying a new pair of shoes and never having to worry about buying another one because every day, this new pair looks as good as the first day you bought it. In the same way, God's love for you never wears out and He will never stop loving you.

As you step out today, keep preaching this truth to yourself. Hold on tightly to it and never let it go. Always remember that God is faithful and He loves you.

Prayer: *Heavenly Father, thank You for Your amazing love for me which never ends. Please help me to always remember that no matter where I find myself, I can always run back into Your arms where Your love is as fresh as ever. In Jesus' name. Amen.*

Today's affirmation: *God will never stop loving me.*

Day 7: Changes

> The grass withers and the flowers fall, but the word of our God endures forever
>
> Isaiah 40:8

Outpourings Of A Beloved Heart

The sun rises and then it sets

The sky brightens and then darkens

The weather always changes

But You never change at all

The flowers bloom and then wither

The rain falls and then it stops

The seasons always change

But You never change at all

People grow taller and people shrink

People beard and others go bald

People come and people go

But You never change at all

Snap backs might be hated today and loved tomorrow

Big lips might be scorned today and praised tomorrow

Society and culture always changes

But You never change at all

For You are not like the changing seasons

Neither are You like the indecisive weather

Your character does not waver

And Your love for me never changes at all

Reflections

Scripture: Isaiah 40:6-8

On my way home from grocery shopping one day, I heard a very deep male voice coming from behind me which I figured was from someone on the phone. As this person slowly walked past me, I realised it was my younger brother's friend but I had been unable to recognise his voice because it had changed so much from the last time I had spoken to him.

When I first met him six years earlier, he was only about nine years old and the high pitched voice he had then sounded nothing like the deep voice I heard that day. This made me realise how much everything is changing in the world around us.

Every time I see a beautiful sunset and I whip out my phone to take a photo, the more time I waste trying to take the perfect photo, the more the sun sets and the more the view changes. Every day is different and seasons are different.

As the years pass, people grow up, get married, some make new friends and many move on. People's feelings can change, relationships break down and some new bonds are formed. Technology is always changing, physical appearances change and our characters can also change.

Outpourings Of A Beloved Heart

Trying to keep up with all of these changes around us can be hard. However, it is comforting to know that we have that one constant thing we can rely on and that is God's love for us. **Hebrews 13:8** tells us that Jesus Christ is the same yesterday, today and forever. Just as we mentioned before that His love is renewed every morning, we can amplify that truth with confidence and say that His love for us never changes.

Never will we wake up one morning to find that God fell out of love with us or that His love has suddenly grown cold. The God we serve today is the same God of Abraham, Isaac and Jacob. His character is still the same. His word has not changed and He is still merciful and loving.

The fact that God does not change means that we can gladly rely on Him because He will never let us down. **The only confidence we have lies in the faithfulness of God's character and if God wasn't faithful, we will have no confidence at all.**

As you step out today, remember that **the Almighty God you read about in the Bible, is the same God we speak about today.** He has not changed. He never will and He still loves you.

Prayer: *Heavenly Father, thank You so much for Your unchanging nature. Thank You that I can rely on Your faithfulness in the past because that is who You are. Please help me to believe with all my heart that You will never let me down. In Jesus' name. Amen.*

Today's affirmation: *God's love for me will never change.*

Questions to think about

> What have you learnt so far about God's character?

PART TWO:
OUR DISOBEDIENT NATURE

"But God showed His great love for us by sending Christ to die for us while we were still sinners."

Romans 5:8 (NLT)

Day 8: Your Love Don't Care

Outpourings Of A Beloved Heart

Your love don't care

It don't care about my skin colour, my body shape or my hair type

Your love don't care about my outward appearance

For You love me just as You made me

Your love don't care

It don't care about my mistakes or my shortcomings

Your love don't care about what I've done

For You have never condemned me and You never will

Your love don't care

It don't care that I was a wretch undeserving of You

You took me in and washed me white as snow

You are gentle with me and You comfort my tired and weary soul

Your love don't care

It don't care that I was lost in the world

For You are my shepherd and I was Your lost sheep

But now, I am no longer lost Lord

You have guided my wandering feet back into Your loving arms

# Reflections

Scripture: John 8:1-11

A while ago, I had a conversation with a first year student at my university. I was telling her about our Christian Union meetings and how it would be great if she came along to one of them. She politely declined my invitation and the reason she gave me was that she didn't feel God would love someone like her.

She went on to explain that she had done some "not so good" things in the past and did not believe God was interested in her. It broke my heart to hear her say those things and it breaks my heart even more to know that there are a lot of people who believe this lie. The lie that they are not good enough to be loved by God.

The story in **John 8** tells of a woman who had been caught in adultery and who was about to face the consequences of her actions. The teachers of religious law had already judged her and found her guilty so they brought her to Jesus. Their intention was to trap Jesus into condemning her but His response in this situation shows another amazing aspect of His love for us. It knows no bounds. (**Romans 3:21-22**).

The woman had been condemned to death by stoning and Jesus asked the person who knew they had never sinned to cast the first stone. What happened next was amazing because one by one, these religious leaders put down their stones and left. They knew they had sinned too and that they were in no position to judge her. The only man who has ever walked the face of the earth, blameless and sinless is Jesus Christ. He was the only one who had the right to condemn her. But He didn't.

Outpourings Of A Beloved Heart

So after the woman's accusers had left, Jesus asked her,

"Where are your accusers? Didn't even one of them condemn you?"

"No Lord," she said.

And Jesus replied, "Neither do I. Go and sin no more."

(John 8:10-11)

God does not really care about your social background, the number of clothes or shoes you own, the kind of degree you have, your job, whether or not you are single or married and He sure does not care about what you have done in the past. He wants you to come to Him as you are- with all your flaws and imperfections.

The woman in this story probably thought it was the end of the road for her. In the eyes of her accusers, she did not deserve forgiveness but it was at this darkest and loneliest moment of her life that Jesus stepped in and showed her love. He gave her comfort, hope and a reason to live again.

Jesus did not do this because of anything the woman had done. No. He did not do it because she deserved forgiveness. No. Jesus saved her because He is merciful and He is the forgiver of all our sins. That is who He is. (**Titus 3:4-7**).

It is important to note that after Jesus forgave her sins, He urged her to go and sin no more. God does not only forgive us but He also gives us the power to sin no more. He transforms our hearts and works within us so we do not go back to the way we were without Him.

Romans 5:8 tells us that Jesus died for us whilst we were still sinners. **If He was looking for righteous, worthy people then**

Outpourings Of A Beloved Heart

He never would have come in the first place. Jesus came to mend the broken-hearted, to heal the sick and to save the lost. Nothing can separate you from His love. Not the pimples on your face, not your skin colour, not your hair type and not even those mistakes you have made.

Have you ever believed the lie that you are not good enough to be loved by God? That you are too messy to be cleansed? Do you ever think that the things you have done make you so "dirty" that He will not be able to wash you white as snow? **God knew how messy you were going to be from the beginning of time and He still declared that He wanted YOU.** Yes, you. He chose you to be part of His family. He chose you because He loves you.

Prayer: *Heavenly Father, thank You so much that Your love for me knows no bounds. I come before You today just as I am because I know that You will never condemn me. I pray that You help me to always remember that You alone have accepted me into Your family because You love me. In Jesus' name. Amen.*

Today's affirmation: *God has chosen me to be part of His family. His love for me knows no bounds.*

Day 9: Rescue Me Lord

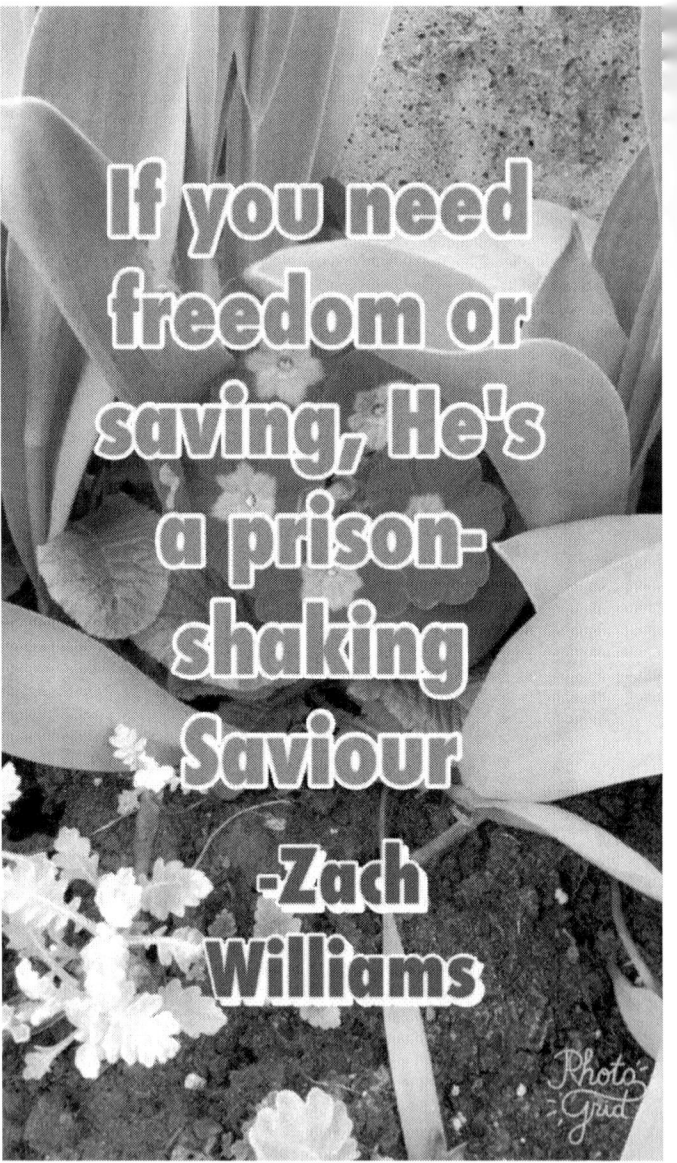

Outpourings Of A Beloved Heart

Rescue me Lord

From this desire to rebel against You

Rescue me from this turbulent wind

That tries to take me away from You

Rescue me Lord

From this urge to do what does not glorify You

Rescue me from the urge

To run after the things You hate

Day after day I tell myself

Soon, very soon, my victory will come

That I will get myself through this

But I have constantly set myself up for failure

Because I have been fighting this on my own

Now I know I have no strength, I need you

For I fight not against flesh and blood

I fight against principalities and powers

And against rulers of the darkness of this world

I fight against spiritual wickedness in high places

Outpourings Of A Beloved Heart

My flesh tries to enslave me

But my soul cries out in despair for freedom

These chains are too heavy for me to bear

I can't move, I can't breathe, I can't live

Please rescue me Lord

Take away my shame and my filth

Take away my anger and my pride

Take away my hatred and my immorality

Please rescue me Lord

For all I want is You

You- my Saviour who breaks every chain

You bring my knees down before You

And when Your Spirit takes over me,

Even my flesh in its rebellion does not stand a chance

For You are still King of kings

And You are Lord of lords

The One bigger than my flesh

The Author and Finisher of my faith

Outpourings Of A Beloved Heart

Change my heart to know You Lord

And bring me to the light of Your Word

May I never go back to living in darkness

Let me know the power of Your resurrection

That I may remain in Your presence and dwell on Your precepts

Meditating on Your Word day and night

Let me be like a tree

Planted by the rivers of water

With leaves that are ever green and prosperous

Let it be restored unto me this day

The joy of my salvation

So that my mouth may sing praises to You

And that my whole being may worship You

May I become more like You

And may I remember now and forever more

That Your love alone has qualified me

Reflections

Scripture: Romans 7:14-25

The Bible tells us that the nature of the flesh is to rebel against God. The flesh does not do what the spirit wants and there is a constant battle between our desires to do the things that please our flesh and our desires to do the things that please God (**Galatians 5:17**).

The Apostle Paul also talked about his own desire to do the things he did not want to do because of the sin living in him. The problem is not that we are tempted because even Jesus was tempted by the devil (**Matthew 4:1-11**). The problem is that it is easier to yield in to those temptations than to flee. It may seem like we are powerless and that there is absolutely no way of escape when we are faced with temptations but that is exactly where Jesus comes in.

The Bible teaches that God does not tempt us (**James 1:13**) but we are lured away by our disobedient nature. Temptations work with our desires to do wrong. They are a perfect duo that lure us into sin. However, it is not a hopeless situation when we are tempted because God understands that we have desires to do wrong and He always shows us a way of escape.

If we yield to the desires of our flesh, we move away from God but if we run after the things of the spirit, we get closer to Him. Jesus came to teach us how to starve our flesh and feed our spirit. When we were lost in the world, we had no hope and no one to save us from our destructive disobedient nature. But through Jesus Christ, we are no longer bound to those chains because Jesus has freed us.

Outpourings Of A Beloved Heart

Are there times when you find yourself deeply rooted in doing wrong things and you desperately need someone to get you out? Have you been struggling with anger, pride, lust or even sexual sin? You cannot fight this battle on your own.

In order for the chains of sin to be broken, you must first recognise the sin living in you. You must also learn to be vulnerable, open up about your struggles and seek help from God. You may also find it useful to find a spiritual mentor or any other trust-worthy person who will pray with you and also hold you accountable.

Jesus is the only One who can save you from the chains of the enemy. He is the One that can deliver you when temptations come. You have freedom in Jesus so cry out to Him today. He will show you a way out. He loves you.

Prayer: *Heavenly Father, thank You so much that You know the struggles I face with dealing with temptations. I know You understand what I feel and only You can give me the strength to overcome. Help me today Lord not to yield to the desires of my flesh. Help me to feed my spirit so I may grow closer to You. In Jesus' name. Amen.*

Today's affirmation: *I am no longer a slave to sin. Jesus has broken my chains.*

Questions to think about

> What are some of the things you are struggling with? What have you learnt about how God's love can help you overcome? What actions will you take to help you overcome?

....
....
....
....
....
....
....
....
....
....
....
....
....
....
....
....
....
....
....

PART THREE:

OUR RESCUE

"For God so loved the world that He gave His one and only Son, that whoever believes in Him shall not perish but have eternal life"

John 3:16 (NIV)

Day 10: Blessed Baby Jesus

> The Son of Man did not come to be served but to serve, and to give His life a ransom for many
>
> Matthew 20:28

Outpourings Of A Beloved Heart

On that holy night in Bethlehem

While shepherds watched their flock

Good tidings of great joy filled the air

For it was the birth of blessed baby Jesus

His coming had been prophesied by many

And that long awaited moment had finally come

Even gold, frankincense and myrrh were not enough

To give the proper worship due unto blessed baby Jesus

There in that manger lay the Saviour of the world

He came to share our in our sufferings

He was the embodiment of the Father's love

And His glory was seen right there in blessed baby Jesus

The world did not recognise Him

But He never came to condemn it

All our hope, peace and joy lay right there in that manger

In the heart of blessed baby Jesus

Reflections

Scripture: Philippians 2:1-11

Many of us may struggle with pride which is when we think of ourselves more highly than others. We may often feel that we deserve to be treated differently because we have better accessories or are more qualified. The problem with focusing on this is that it can easily bring an egotistical mind set and pride makes us want to separate ourselves from things or people that we do not consider to be "like us". Pride can also affect our relationships with others and how we treat people.

One person that absolutely did not care for this idea was Jesus Christ. The Bible passage tells us that He had the very nature of God and in fact, He is, God Himself. He has all the riches we could only ever dream of having and everything on earth and in heaven belongs to Him **(Psalm 24:1)** but He never ever tried to use His supremacy as an excuse to be proud.

He decided to leave His glorious throne in heaven and He willingly made Himself poor because of us. He reduced Himself to nothing so He could come down to earth and be born of a woman- His own creation. And as if that was not enough, He not only humbled himself to have the appearance and the nature of a man, but He also was obedient even to death on the cross.

I had the opportunity to talk about Jesus with a Muslim friend of mine and one of the things she struggled to understand was why Jesus had to leave His throne to become a man. "Didn't that strip Him off His title as God?" she asked. I told her that **no one in heaven or on earth is capable of stripping**

Outpourings Of A Beloved Heart

Him off His title. God is God all by Himself and He is sovereign.

So although it might seem very unnecessary to many, this single act of willingly leaving His throne and coming down to earth speaks volumes about the kind of love He has for us. Jesus came down to earth because He wanted to share in our sufferings. He deliberately made Himself poor so that we might become rich in Him (**2 Corinthians 8:9**). He gave up His riches and came to earth so that we might have those riches in abundance.

What exactly does this mean? It means that because of what Jesus did, you have been made rich in Christ. I am not talking about mere earthly riches. No. I am talking about the heavenly inheritance that we are now entitled to because we have been made children of God through Jesus. It is the Father's pleasure to freely give us the kingdom because of Jesus **(Luke 12:32).**

As you go through today, remember how Jesus humbled himself for you. Think about that when you relate with those around you. Use it as an example in your relationships with others as well. Humble yourself before others just as Jesus humbled himself for you. He loves you.

Prayer: *Heavenly Father, thank You so much for leaving Your throne above to come down to earth for me. I did not deserve it Lord but You did it anyway because You love me. Please help me to show this same kind of love to others around me and not to look at myself as better than others. In Jesus' name. Amen.*

Today's Affirmation: *Jesus became poor so than I might become rich in Him.*

Day 11: The One My Heart Loves

Outpourings Of A Beloved Heart

Let me tell you about the life of a man

A man who came to die for me

Let me tell you about the life of a man

A man who came to give me a reason to live

You see He is spotless, holy and without blemish

Yet He left His throne above so I would not perish

He came down to earth to save a wretch like me

For I was stuck in sin and disobedience I could not see

As a helpless babe that night He came

Emmanuel- God with us, is His name

The light He shone became a light to my path

Yes, He came to steer me away from wrath

He showed me the meaning of true love

For He showered me with love from above

He showed me how to be one with the Father

And as for going back to sin, I did not bother

He showed me I am the apple of His eye

Outpourings Of A Beloved Heart

But the cost to take me away from destruction was high

All He ever wanted was to have my heart

So that in eternity we will never be apart

On the cross of Calvary He went to pay the price for me

He bled, wept and prayed for me

He became sin itself which He had not

And through His precious blood- eternal life I got

On that cross He took His last breath

But He rose again in victory and defeated death

He is coming back again to take me home

So I will worship with Him at the Father's throne

I have been asked why He had to leave His throne for me

I have been asked if it was necessary for Him to die for me

What kind of God does that for His creation?

What kind of God puts Himself in such a humbling situation?

And never ever have I been so confident in the answer

That He did it because He loves me

And friends, if He can love a wretch like me

Then I bring you good news, because He loves you too

So come, come and see the man

Come and see the One my heart loves

Jesus Christ is the man

And He is the One my heart loves

Reflections

Scripture: Romans 5:6-11

God's amazing plan to save us from sin and destruction didn't just end with sending Jesus to share in our sufferings. God's plan was not to provide a temporary solution. It was a plan to save us totally and completely and to give us life for eternity (**John 10:10**). The Bible teaches that there is only one way we can get this eternal life. Only one way to get to the Father and spend eternity with Him. That way is through Jesus alone (**1 John 5:12-13**).

The most important question to think about now is why Jesus is the only way. Why do we have to believe in Jesus to be saved? Why do we have to believe that He is our Lord and Saviour before we can gain access to this eternal life God has promised us? Was the cross necessary? Did He have to die so that we could be saved? The simple answer to the last two questions is YES. **The cross was very necessary.** Yes, He had to die so that we could be saved. We would not be where we

Outpourings Of A Beloved Heart

are today if Jesus did not willingly offer Himself as a sacrifice and here is the reason why.

Before Jesus came, we were lost in the world. Our lives without Him were hopeless. We were strangers to God's love and His promises (**Ephesians 2:11-13).** We were so deeply embedded in our disobedience that we were far away from God. We were in our most rebellious state and had wronged God. A price had to be paid and a sacrifice had to be made to take God's wrath away from us. He is a holy and a just God and He does not tolerate sin. The wages of sin is death **(Romans 6:23)** so someone had to die to blot out all our transgressions. Jesus willingly gave Himself up for us.

In **Leviticus 16,** we read about the Day of Atonement which was an important day for the Israelites in the days of Moses. It was a very special occasion held every year where all the sins of the Israelites were placed on a goat known as the "scapegoat". This goat was then set free into the wilderness carrying God's wrath with it. In this way, the children of Israel did not suffer God's wrath because all their sins had been taken away and placed on the scapegoat. This was the same thing that took place on the cross of Calvary, except it wasn't a goat hanging on the cross-but the Son of God and the light of the world.

The big difference between Jesus' sacrifice and the goat used in Moses' time is that Jesus only had to die once and all our sins were wiped away. All the sins we have ever committed or will ever commit were placed on Jesus. Our sins weren't only placed on Him, but **He became sin itself** even though He had never sinned. He took God's wrath upon Himself and bore all our suffering and shame. And He did not stay dead but He rose again in victory and defeated death. **If death**

(which happens to be our greatest fear) had no power over Him, then what can hold Him down? Absolutely nothing at all.

So why is Jesus the only way? Because of what He did on the cross. No one else went through that for you. Jesus did and He did it willingly. Because of Jesus, there is no more wrath. You are now seen as blameless, flawless and righteous in God's eyes. Jesus gave you that righteousness. The cross was necessary for you. It was necessary for you to be part of God's family. It was necessary because God loves you.

If you take some time to meditate on this, then you will realise how amazing it is. As you go through today, remember that Jesus has already paid the price for you. **You can confidently approach God's throne knowing that Jesus has saved you**. **There is no more wrath**. He loves you.

Prayer: *Heavenly Father, thank You so much for sending Your only Son Jesus to die for me. Thank You for taking away all my sins and for making me right with You. Help me to always remember the significance of what You did for me on the cross. In Jesus' name. Amen.*

Today's Affirmation: *Jesus paid the price for me. There is no more wrath.*

Day 12: Your Grace

Outpourings Of A Beloved Heart

Grace is You choosing to love me

I was a liar and a cheat,

My thoughts were dirty and impure

And my feet took me far away into the world

But You still chose to love me

Grace is You choosing to love me

I lived life believing everything else but the truth

I thought I knew it all and didn't need You

And my whole being ached to disobey You

But You still chose to love me

Grace is You loving the unlovely

Yes, even one as unlovely as me

Grace is Your unmerited favour towards me

It is You choosing to love even me

For You are God and You are supreme

And You show mercy to whomever You please

You have the power to choose me or discard me

And yet, every day, You still choose to love me

Reflections

Scripture: Ephesians 2:1-10

I am always amazed whenever I think about God's grace and what it means for us. I stand amazed when I think about what His grace saved us from. **God's grace is unmerited favour**. It is favour from God for which we will never be able to work for. Grace flows freely from God's throne and He has given it to us as a gift because of the love He has for us.

God's grace helps us in time of need and it is only because of it that we have been saved from death (**Ephesians 2:8**). His grace strengthens our hearts (**Hebrews 13:9**) and He has apportioned this grace to each and every one of us (**Ephesians 4:7**).

Grace covers a multitude of sins (**1 Peter 4:8**). We have been forgiven of every sin because of God's grace if we believe. **Grace however, is not and will never be an excuse for sin** (**Romans 6:1**). If we truly understand that God has rescued us, made us alive in Christ and qualified us to be His beloved ones, then we would not want to take advantage of His love.

The Bible teaches that our salvation came because God decided to show us special favour. It is not based on our works because if it were, then we will only boast in ourselves. It is not a reward for the good things we have done so we can't take credit for it. **Our salvation is by God's grace alone and through faith in Christ Jesus.**

By His grace, sin can no longer be our master (**Romans 6:14**), we are free from the chains of the enemy. This grace is sufficient for us through every circumstance we face (**2 Corinthians 12:9**) and grace will keep us to the end.

So today, if the enemy tries to bring in lies and deceit to try and bring the past to haunt you, point him to the cross. The tomb is still empty. Jesus is alive and you are highly favoured. You are looked after and you are loved by Him.

Prayer: *Dear Heavenly Father, thank You so much for Your grace which You have freely given me. I know that I will never be able to earn it but You have given me because You love me. Help me Lord not to take advantage of it but to live my life for You. In Jesus' name. Amen.*

Today's affirmation: *I have been saved by God's grace alone and through faith in Christ Jesus.*

Day 13: In Your Presence

Outpourings Of A Beloved Heart

When I am in Your presence,

Everything feels just right

I find everything I need

I find comfort for my weary soul

I find peace that transcends all understanding

When I am in Your presence,

My faith is renewed

My broken heart is mended

My purpose is made clear

My joy is complete

When I am in Your presence,

Everything makes sense

Your love captivates me

I never want to leave

I'll stay right here at your feet Lord

So I can fully savour the wondrousness

Of Your glorious presence

Outpourings Of A Beloved Heart

Reflections

Scripture: Matthew 27:45-54

So far, we have seen how significant Jesus' death on the cross was and why it was necessary for Him to die for us. We now know that Jesus died to pay the price for our sins and also to make us right with God. One other thing Jesus' death and resurrection brought us is freedom to access God's presence.

Before Jesus died, the temple in Jerusalem was the dwelling place for God's presence. Following on from the laws given to Moses, all the animal sacrifices had to take place in this temple and they were performed by the high priests. There was a special part of the temple called the "Holy of Holies" and this was the exact place where God's presence was (**Hebrews 9:1-3**).

It was separated from the other parts of the temple by a thick curtain and only the high priests were allowed to go in once a year to make atonement for the sins of the people (**Exodus 30:10**). This meant that the people were separated from God's presence because of their sins and they could not enter the "Holy of Holies" (**Isaiah 59:1-2**). This has been the Jewish custom right from the days of Moses.

Everything changed the very moment Jesus died on the cross. **Matthew 27:51** tells us that this thick curtain that guarded the Holy of Holies in the temple was torn in two all the way from top to bottom. The significance of this was that Jesus' death took away that barrier between us and God's presence and so we now have access. Jesus' death was the perfect sacrifice and so no more sacrifices have to be made to make atonement for our sins. The curtains that were torn represented His flesh which was broken for our sake. Jesus

Outpourings Of A Beloved Heart

paved the way for us to get to the Father (**Hebrews 10:19-20**) so we are no longer separated from Him.

Because Jesus died, we do not need any one carrying our prayers to God. He has given us the privilege to pray to Him freely without ceasing (**1 Thessalonians 5:17**). We can sing praises to Him for as long as we want. We can pour out our hearts to Him ourselves and He will always listen to us. His presence dwells among us and Jesus Himself lives within us so we have all we need because we have Jesus.

As God's beloved ones, we need to constantly seek His presence. In **Exodus 33:15**, Moses pleaded with God not to let him go anywhere without His presence because Moses knew that God's presence brings favour and it was what distinguished the Israelites from other people.

You have the privilege to have an intimate relationship with your Heavenly Father. You can know Him for yourself and work out your own salvation with fear and trembling. **Everything you need is in the presence of God** so never stop spending time with Him and feasting on His word because God delights in and takes pleasure in those who seek Him with all their hearts. As you step out today, remember that you have access to God's presence through Christ Jesus and His presence will never leave you. He loves you.

Prayer: *Heavenly Father, thank You for loving me so much that You decided to give me access to Your presence through Jesus. Thank You because I am no longer separated from You. Please help me remember that Your presence is always with me and will never leave me. In Jesus' name. Amen.*

Today's affirmation: *I will never stop seeking the presence of God.*

Outpourings Of A Beloved Heart

Questions to think about

> What have you learnt about the significance of Jesus' coming to earth and dying on the cross for you?

....
....
....
....
....
....
....
....
....
....
....
....
....
....
....
....
....
....
....

PART FOUR:

OUR IDENTITY

"But you are a chosen people, a royal priesthood, a holy nation, God's special possession, that you may declare the praises of Him who called you out of darkness into His marvellous light."

1 Peter 2:9 (NIV)

"Yet to all who received Him, to those who believed in His name, He gave the right to become children of God"

John 1:12 (NIV)

Day 14: Not Good Enough?

Outpourings Of A Beloved Heart

My mind streams with ideas and thoughts

My mouth itches to let the words out

But in fear, I hold them back and pout

Because in my head I hear the voices shout

"You are not good enough"

I see others excel in life

I want to believe that I too can thrive

That I too can reach those heights

But in my head I hear the voices sigh

"You are not good enough"

I have dreams and I have hopes

The little ones and the big ones

I have strengths and I have goals

But in my head I hear the voices moan

"You are not good enough"

I want to achieve and be better

I want to be accepted and not be bitter

But in my head I still hear the voices utter

Outpourings Of A Beloved Heart

"You are not good enough"

So I let the thoughts sink in
I start to let the fear creep in
I walk away and abandon my dreams
I repeat those words to myself and I give in
"I am not good enough"

But wait a minute, their opinion does not matter
Because I know the God who created matter
I know the One who gave me those thoughts
I know the One who made my mouth
For He put those words in my mouth to shout

I know the One who gave me those desires
The One who kept me unharmed through the fire
I know the One who has given me hope
The One who refines me to be as pure as gold

My God knows I have these doubts
And only He can get them out

Outpourings Of A Beloved Heart

So no, their opinion does not matter

Because to Him, I matter

So then my soul, I implore you to run wild

For you were not just made to survive but to thrive

Listen to the Father's love crying out

He has always loved you without a doubt

You have Jesus and He is enough

Reflections

Scripture: 1 Peter 2:4-10

I remember the day I wrote this poem. It had been a really rough day and things weren't going as I had planned. I thought the day had started off well and I thought I knew what I was doing but I realised later on that I had absolutely no idea. I tried so hard to motivate myself to keep going but the negative thoughts started creeping in.

The voices in my head told me I was stupid. They told me I was never going to achieve what I was aiming for. They told me to quit and that I was wasting my time. I broke down and cried because I felt really discouraged. When I finally went home to seek answers from God, He encouraged me with His word from **1 Peter 2:9-10**. It was while I was meditating on this scripture that I was inspired to write this poem.

Outpourings Of A Beloved Heart

We will have to battle with negative thoughts at some point in our lives. These thoughts can be discouraging and can make us lose the confidence we have in Christ. They can also bring doubt and make us start to question our worth and our purpose in life.

But when these thoughts come, we need to remember what God thinks about us. **1 Peter 2:9** reminds us that we are precious to God. He calls us beloved which means He loves and cherishes us very dearly (**1 Thessalonians 1:4). God loves us as much as He loves Jesus** (**John 17:22-23**). Do you believe that with all your heart?

Dealing with discouragement may be a constant battle and it is not easy but it is very possible with the strength we have in Christ. We need to know the truth about ourselves and this truth will set us free from the lies of the enemy. Here are some important truths to remember when you feel discouraged and when you feel you are not good enough.

You have been chosen by Jesus (**John 15:16**)

God has a plan for you and He created you with a purpose (**Jeremiah 29:11**)

You have been empowered and you can do all things through Christ who strengthens you (**Philippians 4:13**)

You are beautiful inside out (**Psalm 45:11**)

You are a child of God (**John 1:12**)

You are unique (**Psalm 139:13**)

You are loved (**Jeremiah 31:3**)

You are part of God's family (**Ephesians 2:19**)

Outpourings Of A Beloved Heart

You are precious in God's eyes (**1 Corinthians 6:20**)

You have been forgiven (**Colossians 1:14**)

You are free from condemnation (**Romans 8:1**)

You are cared for since conception (**Ephesians 3:17-19**)

You are the temple of God's Holy Spirit (**1 Corinthians 3:16**)

You are Jesus' friend (**John 15:15**)

You belong to God (**Isaiah 43:1**)

Your value and worth are in Christ. Your identity is in Christ alone. When you do not know your worth in Christ, it would be very easy for your faith to be crippled. It would be easy to let other things and people define who you are. Don't let the discouragements from the world bring you down. It's not up to the world to decide who you are. **You don't have to guess who you are because God has already given you an identity.**

You may be in the world but you are not of the world. **Jesus paid a high price to make you different from the world**. The negative thoughts may come but you can overcome them when you stand firm on Christ, the solid rock. He loves you.

Prayer: *Heavenly Father, thank You so much for the person You have made me to be. Help me Lord to always remember my worth and identity in You. Help me not to become discouraged when faced with negative thoughts. Please strengthen me Lord so that I may continue to live life for Your glory. In Jesus' name. Amen.*

Today's Affirmation: *I belong to God. He has chosen me. I am valued. I am precious. I am loved.*

Questions to think about

> What have you learnt about your identity, worth and value?

PART FIVE:
OUR PURPOSE

"For by Him all things were created, in heaven and on earth, visible and invisible, whether thrones and or dominions or rulers or authorities- all things were created through Him and for Him."

Colossians 1:16

Day 15: I Bow My Head In Worship

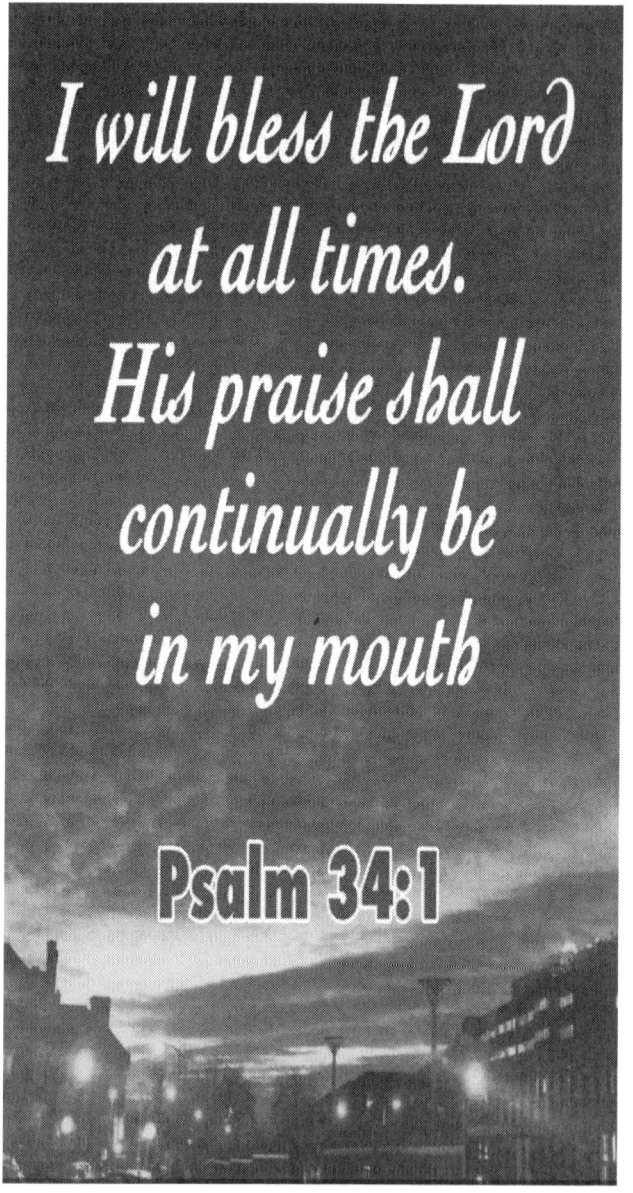

Outpourings Of A Beloved Heart

I come into Your loving presence

To worship the Holy One of Israel

I bow my head in reverence

Because I want the full experience

Confidently, I come before You

Your throne of grace draws me in

With my hands lifted up, I exalt You

For because of You, I live

I lift my eyes to seek Your loving face

Tears of joy fall softly down my cheeks

For You alone are my dwelling place

And all about Your love I boldly speak

With all my heart, I extol You

Over the earth, Your beautiful name I proclaim

My mouth sings unending praises to You

I bow in worship to You without restraint

With all that I am, I give glory to You

Outpourings Of A Beloved Heart

My whole being worships You for who You are

For I live and move and have my being in You

So I worship You Lord- always and forever

Reflections

Scripture: John 4:21-26

During our weekly Christian Union meetings at university, we have worship sessions which I always look forward to. These sessions involve singing songs and playing instruments like the guitar, piano and the cajón. It's always lovely to see how everyone gets into it with some hands lifted high and some eyes closed. Most people always seem to be lost in the moment and I love the atmosphere it brings with it.

While growing up, I always thought worship was all about singing songs to God and perhaps you too may think the same. **Although singing songs to God is an expression of worship, it is not a definition of worship.** The Bible urges us to worship God in spirit and in truth but we can't understand what that means if we do not first understand what true worship is.

True worship is when we come to acknowledge that God alone is Lord of our lives. It comes with the realisation that God comes first and that He deserves the number one place in our hearts. It is an act of reverence and adoration and it is not only about acknowledging what God has done but simply acknowledging that He alone is God.

True worship is acknowledging the great love God has for us and living our lives in submission to Him. **It is a lifestyle that involves reverence for God and His word in everything that we do**.

True worship is how we treat others and how we reflect the love God has shown us. It comes from a heart that has been renewed by the acknowledgement of God's love. So if we have not come to that place where we can totally submit everything to Him through our lifestyle, then the songs we sing will be nothing but empty words.

What did Jesus mean when He said true worshippers must worship in spirit and in truth? (**John 4:23**). The **"truth"** part of this verse is referring to the truth of the gospel. We worship God in truth when we accept that Jesus is our personal Lord and Saviour because He is the Word (**John 1:14**), the way, the truth and the life (**John 14:6**).

To worship God "**in spirit**" means we abandon our old lifestyle and embrace our new lifestyle being led by the spirit. Being born again means we have been born of the spirit and not the flesh. It means we abandon the ways of the flesh and live by the spirit. Only those who have been made alive in Christ can worship Him in spirit. (**John 3:3, 3:5-8**).

True worship is an experience propelled by the Holy Spirit who works within us and opens our eyes to see the beauty of Christ. It doesn't only end with singing songs to God. Worshipping God is an everyday thing. We should worship God when we go out, when we come in and when we lay down. We should worship Him in what we say, where we go and what we think. Worship is about focusing on Jesus and it is an outpouring of the love we have for Him. **We only love God because He has loved us first.**

Outpourings Of A Beloved Heart

So as you step out today, seek to worship God through your lifestyle in spirit and in truth. **You don't only have to wait to sing "Oceans" or "Reckless Love" before you acknowledge that God loves you.** Let the songs you sing to Him not be empty words but let your heart truly acknowledge Him as the loving God over your life. He loves you.

Prayer: *Heavenly Father, thank You for all that You are. I acknowledge the fact that You are Lord over all things and Lord of my life. Receive all the glory You deserve now and forever. In Jesus' name. Amen.*

Today's Affirmation: *I will be a true worshipper and worship God in spirit and in truth.*

Day 16: I Give You All Of Me

Outpourings Of A Beloved Heart

Take my hands Lord

I give them to you

Take these hands of mine

And use them to do work endlessly for You

Take my feet Lord

I surrender them to You

Take these feet that often wander away from You

Let them walk and run every day for You

Take my tongue Lord

I give it to You

Take this tongue that has the power of life and death

And let it speak, sing and shout praises to You

Take my feelings and my emotions Lord

I give them to you

These feelings and emotions that can blind me

Teach me not to let these come before You

Take my heart Lord

Outpourings Of A Beloved Heart

I give it to you

Take this disobedient heart of mine

And transform it to love like You

Take all of me Lord

I give You all of me

Draw me closer and closer to You

For my earnest desire is to love and be loved by You

Reflections

Scripture: Mark 10:17-31

So far, we have learnt that true worship comes from a heart that has acknowledged God's sovereign love and one that has accepted Christ as personal Lord and Saviour. In order to completely do this, we need to surrender everything to God. Surrendering is one thing we may struggle with in our Christian walk but it is a very necessary component.

If we examine ourselves carefully, we may find that we are not very different from the rich man in the Bible passage. This man obeyed every single commandment and he considered himself blameless before the law so he came to Jesus, desperate to know what else he could do to gain eternal life. However, Jesus challenged him regarding the way he looked at salvation.

Outpourings Of A Beloved Heart

When Jesus asked the man to sell all his possessions and give the money to the poor, he became deeply saddened because he had great wealth (**Mark 10:22**). In other words, this was an area in the man's life he had come to love more than he loved Jesus. He was not willing to give it up for the sake of Christ and just like this man, a lot of us today might still be holding on to things in our lives that prevent us from totally surrendering to God.

This passage is not just referring to wealth and riches but everything else that could be an idol in our lives. **An idol would be anything we put before God and anything we love more than Him.** One idol I had in my life was my obsession with being in a relationship. I was so caught up in wanting to be in a relationship that it became all I could think about. God later revealed to me that this was an area I had to completely surrender to Him and to let Him take control. **We cannot say we love God when we put other things before Him.**

God's desire is for us to draw closer to Him each day. He wants us to get to know His character and to be more like Him. In **Romans 12:1-2**, the Apostle Paul wrote a letter to the church in Rome urging them to offer their bodies as a living sacrifice to God- a sacrifice that is holy and acceptable unto Him.

He also encouraged the church to not be conformed to the world but to be transformed by the renewing of their minds. **God's love comes with transformation.** You are never the same when you fully grasp the magnitude of His love. You don't think like the world, your priorities change and most of all, you discover your purpose on earth which is to love and be loved by Him.

Outpourings Of A Beloved Heart

In order for us to discover what God's good and perfect will is, we need to surrender our will first. By being deeply rooted in His word, we allow Him to renew our minds and work in our hearts so that we will become set apart as holy unto Him. In order for our minds to be renewed, we need to die to ourselves so we may start to bear the fruits of the spirit and become witnesses to the world.

My good friend- Jessica, told me about another way to look at the act of surrendering. She said that surrendering to God does not mean giving up all our ideas and thoughts but it means exchanging it for something so much better. We naturally always want to hold on to things in our lives that we think are good for us but Jesus came to offer us something so much better. The real question is, are we ready to let go of what we have and let Him take over?

Do you have burdens and worries? Surrender them to Him and He will give you rest and peace. Do you have ideas and dreams? Surrender them to Him and He will reveal to you much greater plans. Do you have emptiness and brokenness? Surrender them to Him and He will fill you with joy and satisfaction.

With Jesus, all things are possible so today, give your all to Him and watch Him use you mightily for His glory. He loves you.

Prayer: *Heavenly Father, thank You for Your amazing love that transforms my heart and mind to be more like You. Teach me today to learn to surrender all that I am so that You may use me for Your glory. In Jesus Name. Amen.*

Today's affirmation: *I will totally and completely surrender my life to Jesus.*

Day 17: The Way Of Life

Outpourings Of A Beloved Heart

As you go through life you'll sense

That life's got just one end

So living in it you have to be careful

And most of all you have to be truthful

Don't always try to please everyone

Because in the end, you'll end up with no one

For you'll never be able to meet all their expectations

Instead, try to please God in every situation

Learn to say no sometimes

Lest they learn to exploit you anytime

In every situation, always be thankful to God, the Father

Coz He knows the whole mystery of the matter

Learn to keep God's commandments

And He, faithful and just will lead you out of your predicaments

Do not yield always to anger

Because right after anger, there's danger

Outpourings Of A Beloved Heart

Let your life be filled with happy moments

And try to cast away the sad torments

Most especially, love the Lord with all your heart, soul and spirit

Because believe it or not, you were born for this

Finally, let the Potter your life mould

Because He has been, He is and will always be in control

Reflections:

Scripture: Colossians 3:12-17

I wrote this poem when I was fourteen years old and every time I read it, I always wonder if I truly understood what it meant to live for God. Maybe I did understand these words and maybe I didn't but I would like to focus on what the Bible says about how we should live as God's beloved ones.

Colossians 1:16 tells us that we were made for God and for His glory. God is the very centre of our lives and He is our purpose. We have seen that the proof of God's love for us was sending His Son- Jesus to die so we can have eternal life. So to show our love for Him, we have to live for Him and obey Him (**John 14:15**).

The Apostle Paul reminded the church in Colossae about living a life as those who have been made alive in Christ. **A heart that has been transformed by God's love bears fruits and by these fruits shall we be known (Matthew 7:16).**

Outpourings Of A Beloved Heart

As God's beloved ones, we have virtues and when we allow the Holy Spirit to work in us, He directs us on how to live according to God's will. **Colossians 3:17** tells us that **the way of life is to give God glory in everything we do**. Not some things. Not when we feel like it but at all times and in everything we do. That is our purpose and that is what we were made for.

A lot of Christians always talk about wanting to find their purpose. How do you find it? How do you know you have found it? Perhaps you reading this have wondered the same thing too? What is your purpose? Well here is an answer for you. **God is your purpose.** That is the reason why the Bible urges you to seek Him first in all that you do. It is the same reason why God wants you to know Him. **If you know God, you know your purpose.**

The Bibles says that as God's beloved one, you are the light of the world and you are like a city that is built on a hill which cannot be hidden. All the talents and gifts God has given you are meant to facilitate this purpose which is to give God glory. As you grow in the knowledge of Him and surrender to Him, He begins to lead you along the path He has purposed for you. **Nothing is more fulfilling than living a life that pleases God.**

Your job here on earth is to represent Jesus to the world. You are upholding His reputation and letting the world see His glory. God's glory is His physical and tangible presence which has been made manifest through our senses so your purpose is to let others see Jesus in you.

For this reason, it is important to check who you are representing to the world because the world is watching. Once you claim to be with Jesus, you can either lead people astray or bring them into the kingdom so **examine yourself always to check that you are still in faith.**

Does that sound like a lot of work? Do you feel under pressure? Remember this will all go wrong when you rely on your own strength. God is the One who is working within you to will and to act according to His good purpose **(Philippians 2:13).** God always provides in order for His will to be done.

Do you put Jesus at the centre of every single thing you do?

Does your life reflect His glory?

Do others see Jesus in you?

As you step out today, commit your words, thoughts and actions into God's hands. Ask the Holy Spirit to work within you and to guide you so that through you, others can see Jesus. He is your purpose and He loves you.

Prayer: *Heavenly Father, thank You for my heart that has been changed by Your love and for continuously pouring out Your love upon me. Help me to always put You at the centre of everything I do so that others can see You in me and glorify You. In Jesus' name. Amen.*

Today's Affirmation: *I will let others see Jesus in me. I must decrease and He must increase.*

Day 18: Doubts

> But when you ask, you must believe and not doubt, because the one who doubts is like a wave of the sea blown and tossed by the wind.
>
> James 1:6

Outpourings Of A Beloved Heart

Fear grips my heart

Doubts flood my mind

Negativity overwhelms me

These thoughts try to make a home

So they can drive You away

So that I may take my eyes off You

And sink deep into these flooding waters of worry

But You oh Lord are my fortress

You are my stronghold and my hope

At the mention of Your name, these doubts flee

Because Your name brings peace and comfort

And in the hollow of Your hands, You hold me

So that I am safe and secure

And I can go to sleep in peace

For You oh Lord never slumber nor sleep

Outpourings Of A Beloved Heart

Reflections

Scripture: 1 Samuel 17: 41-50

The one thing I have struggled with for a long time now is overcoming doubt. Sometimes, I doubt the abilities God has given me and I doubt my calling. Many times, I have also found myself doubting God and His promises. To doubt simply means to "lack confidence in". We can lack confidence in others, in ourselves and we can also lack confidence in God.

Doubts bring unnecessary worry and anxiety. They make us lose trust in God and His love for us. Doubts do not come from God but from the devil. It is the devil's trick to lure us away from what really matters and to make us lose our faith. There are a lot of people who doubted God in the Bible and one of them was Abraham's wife-Sarah.

When God visited Abraham in **Genesis 18**, He promised to give Sarah a son but she found that really hard to believe. She laughed to herself because of how ridiculous it sounded and she doubted God's promise. In the end, we see that God was true to His word and this promise came to pass even though Sarah had believed this to be an impossibility.

The remedy for doubt is faith and an example of someone who acted in a different way to Sarah was David in **1 Samuel 17**. We see in this passage that the children of Israel were being terrorised by the giant Philistine called Goliath. Goliath was confident in his size and his trained skills so he thought no one could possibly take him down.

David was a man after God's own heart and looking a lot smaller, he put his confidence in God. David went out to fight

Goliath with only a stone and sticks. We see that David never doubted God's abilities and neither did he doubt God's power. He was able to step out because he had the confidence that God's mighty power will be seen through Him and with that, Goliath was defeated.

Sometimes, God can give us desires to do certain things but because we doubt His abilities and are not confident enough in what He can use us for, we become complacent and stay in our comfort zones. God works in mighty ways and He wants to use you today for His glory. This message is for you who is reading this right now and for you who is having doubts.

Sarah was old and biologically not able to have children but she did because God was involved. Goliath was big, strong and well trained in war while David was just a shepherd boy who appeared small and weak, but he defeated Goliath because God was involved. Do you see that when God opens the door no one can shut it? And that when He closes a door no one can open it? Is anything too hard for the Lord? Why then do you doubt Him?

What is that thing God has called you to do?

Have you been wanting to write a book?

Did you want to start a blog or a YouTube channel?

What about that business you wanted to start up?

Take an example from David today. Do not be afraid of the "giants" standing before you. They are causing you to doubt what God has in store for you. **Don't let the barriers of men limit God's power in your life.** Instead, step out in confidence and make an impact for His glory. He is always going to be

Outpourings Of A Beloved Heart

ready to use you so make yourself available for Him. He loves you.

Prayer: *Heavenly Father, thank You for the confidence that You have given me in You. I pray Lord Jesus that I will not focus on things that do not matter but that I will believe in the promises You have given me and step out to make an impact for Your glory. In Jesus' name. Amen.*

Today's Affirmation: *I will not doubt God's power and neither will I doubt His abilities. I will not let the barriers of men limit God's power in my life.*

Questions to think about

> What have you learnt about your purpose? Have you discovered your gifts, talents or calling? Are these being used to bring God glory?

PART SIX:

OUR COMFORT

"And after you have suffered a little while, the God of all grace who has called you into His eternal glory in Christ, will Himself restore, confirm, strengthen and establish you."

1 Peter 5:10 (ESV)

Day 19: I Wonder Why

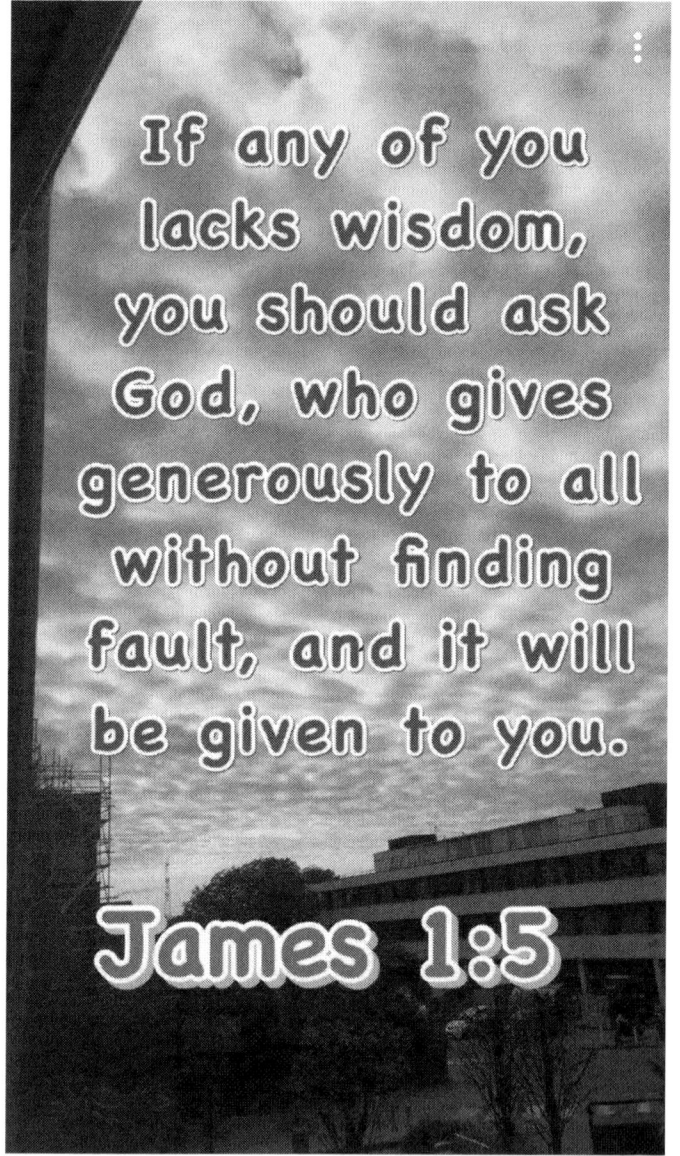

Outpourings Of A Beloved Heart

Many times I've wondered why

I've wondered why You let the pain

And other times I've wondered why

I've wondered if the pain brought me any gain

In my sleepless nights I wondered why

I wondered why You left the mountains unmoved

And in those early mornings, I wondered why

I wondered if there was something You wanted to prove

The pain made no sense

So I wondered why You let it stay

Frustrated with the pain, I took offence

And even with that, You didn't take it away

I know You always mean well

But I'm only human; I cannot see

So please teach me to say "It is well"

And to hope in the glory I cannot see

I want to be strong for You

Outpourings Of A Beloved Heart

But this heart of mine was made to bleed

So let me be strengthened by You

So that these open wounds may heal

I may not understand why

But I know You hold the answer to my uncertainty

If You will, I may keep wondering why

But I know that'll only be as long as I'm on this side of eternity

Reflections:

Scripture: Habakkuk 1:2-5

At the very beginning of this book, we acknowledged the fact that suffering, struggles and pain have consumed the world. Suffering is not something we just watch from a distance but it is something we all go through together (**Romans 8:22-23**). Our individual sufferings may be different in many ways and they may come in very different forms but that does not change the fact that we all do genuinely suffer in one way or another.

Going through storms and trials can leave us with many questions and sometimes it may seem like God is silent. This can leave us in a state of uncertainty where we start to wonder why. When we don't get the answers we want, we can get angry at God and think He does not understand what we are going through. When things do not make sense, the devil can use this as an opportunity to trick us into abandoning God.

We see in the Bible passage that the prophet Habakkuk was also in a position where he had so many questions to ask God. He asked why God was not doing anything about their situation and how long it was going to take before something was done (**Habakkuk 1:2-3**). He had been praying for God to take away the wickedness and injustice in Judah but it seemed like God was silent regarding the matter. We read later on that God heard all of Habakkuk's prayers and He was up to something good (**Habakkuk 1:5**).

James 1:5 tells us that **God gives us wisdom in our trials**. Wisdom gives us the ability to discern what God wants us to do through the guidance of the Holy Spirit. Wisdom enables us to discern the source of our hardships, the purpose for them and also how to respond to them. God might want you to do something, to take a step out in faith or He might just simply want you to keep praying, to keep trusting Him and to keep waiting on Him.

Seeking wisdom during our trials will involve seeking God's face through prayer, fasting, spending time in His word and it may also be through godly counsel. The Bible says when we ask God for wisdom in our trials, He will not resent our asking. **Sometimes, it is when we are lost that we can get a chance to grow and to see who we are and where God really wants us to be.**

Are you in a position where you are struggling to understand a lot of things going on in your life?

Have you found yourself at crossroads with no idea of what to do next or where to go?

Outpourings Of A Beloved Heart

Are you struggling to understand why you have had to go through certain things in your life?

As you step out today, commit to asking God for wisdom when you do not understand. Also remember that someday, you will have the answers to all your questions. Someday, you will understand why so ask Him for wisdom today and He will give it to you. God is still in control and He still loves you.

Prayer: *Heavenly Father, thank You for Your words of encouragement today reminding me that You give wisdom in trials. I hold on to Your word today Lord and I ask that You please give me wisdom to see Your hand working for me even when I do not understand why. In Jesus' name. Amen.*

Today's Affirmation: *God will give me wisdom in my trials.*

Day 20: You Kept Me

> And we know that God causes everything to work together for the good of those who love God and are called according to His purpose
>
> Romans 8:28

Outpourings Of A Beloved Heart

I squeezed through those cracks.

Their sharp edges lacerated my skin.

But boy did I squeeze through tight

And I came out alive.

I was thrown into the fire.

Thrown in head first and I crash landed.

Yes, I was bruised and wounded.

But no, I was not consumed.

I was pressed on every side,

By all the weight that came

From carrying the pressure not to fail.

I was pressed but I was not crushed.

Lord it was only when I was down

That I looked up and saw You.

I saw that You had been involved all along

And that You kept me.

Sliding through those cracks, You kept me.

Outpourings Of A Beloved Heart

Even when I walked through the fire, You kept me.

Lord in the midst of all that pressure, You kept me.

You were shaping my heart to trust You.

You were refining me

To come out as pure gold.

It was as if You were a puppet Master.

Except, You are no puppet Master.

You are the One and only Master Planner.

Reflections:

Scripture: 2 Corinthians 4:7-18

One solid truth about God that I hold very dear to my heart is believing that He is always in control. This truth gives me assurance that my good and loving Father who created the whole universe is in control of everything at all times. I do not only believe this in triumph, when things seem to be going right but also in tragedy, when everything seems to be going wrong. So even when things do not go my way and I face disappointments and rejections, I have come to understand that God's plan is still working.

The Bible teaches in **James 1:2-3** that there is purpose in our trials. **The circumstances we go through do not take God by surprise.** He knows all things and He sees all things (**Hebrews 4:13**). He knew about the trials we were going to face from the beginning of time and He is with us as we go through them.

James 1:2 encourages us to see our trials as an opportunity for great joy because perseverance can only be produced when our faith is tested. It also tells us that trials come to mature us so that we might be complete and lacking nothing. **James 1:12** also tells us that **God delights in and blesses those who persevere when they go through trials**. It says that those who do not lose heart will receive the crown of life.

Romans 8:18 encourages us to see that our sufferings and what we go through on earth can never be compared to all the glory that God will reveal to us later. Even though we are all suffering together, we have great hope for believing in Jesus because we have the confidence that one day, God will take us into the place of complete abundance (**Romans 8:23-25**). God is working everything for our good (**Romans 8:28**) and even though it may not always seem like it, **we have this assurance because we know that He is a good and loving God**.

God is not malicious. He is not a sadist and He does not enjoy causing anyone sorrow **(Lamentations 3:32-33).** His heart breaks when our hearts break and He really does care about what we go through so He gives us strength and power to overcome. **2 Corinthians 4:7-18** teaches that though life may put us through burdensome situations, we are not destroyed because we have Jesus. As long as we fix our eyes on Him, we will be renewed day by day so let us not be weary and heavy hearted. Instead, let us ask God what He is trying to teach us from the situation we are facing.

Outpourings Of A Beloved Heart

Ask God what lesson He wants you to learn from your trial and how it is shaping your heart to be more like Him. Ask that He opens your eyes to see what virtue He is trying to develop in you through your trial? Is it patience? Is it self-control? Perhaps He is trying to teach you the meaning of true joy which enables you to always see the beauty of Christ no matter what you are facing.

Perhaps He wants to teach you to be totally dependent on Him and for Him to do that, He'll have to strip you off everything you've got. Perhaps He wants to show you that His power shines bright in your weakness and for that, He'll have to gracefully break you. You may sorrow, shed tears and go through pain, but please be encouraged in the Lord today and lift up your eyes to Jesus.

Be encouraged that you do not sorrow like one who has no hope. **Your sorrows are not in vain. God is up to something and He is up to something good. He also delights in bringing triumphant victory for His children.** He has brought you this far so He will not let you down. He loves you.

"Therefore, since we have been justified through faith, we have peace with God through our Lord Jesus Christ, through whom we have gained access by faith into this grace in which we now stand. And we boast in the hope of the glory of God. Not only so, but we also glory in our sufferings, because we know that suffering produces perseverance; perseverance, character; and character, hope. And hope does not put us to shame, because God's love has been poured out into our hearts through the Holy Spirit, who has been given to us. "

Romans 5:1-5

Prayer: *Dear Heavenly Father, thank You so much for Your reassurance that my sorrows and sufferings are not in vain. Thank You for the reassurance that You are working out Your plan within me for my own good. Please help me to see what You are trying to teach me and how my trials help me to become more like You. In Jesus' name. Amen.*

Today's Affirmation: *I do not sorrow in vain. There is a purpose for my trials. When God has tested me, I will come forth as pure gold.*

Day 21: Near To My Broken Heart

Outpourings Of A Beloved Heart

You are near to my broken heart

You overwhelm that which overwhelms me

When nothing seems to go right for me

You send Your words to comfort me

You are near to my broken heart

You strengthen me in my weakness

When I am down and faithless

You remind me Your love is endless

You are near to my broken heart

Your yoke is easy and Your burden is light

You never cast me away from Your sight

But the hope and love within me You reignite

You are near to my broken heart

You teach me how to restart

And even when I think we are far apart

You are always near to my broken heart

Reflections

Scripture: Matthew 11:28-30

Have you ever found yourself in a situation that has left you broken hearted? It could be the death of a loved one, going through a bad break up, failures, disappointments, rejections or even the feeling of loneliness. Have you ever felt like you were at your breaking point and ready to throw in the towel? Is there a situation causing you to consider walking away from God?

Be encouraged in the Lord today. The story of Job is one you can draw much encouragement from. Job lost everything God had given Him including all his possessions and his children. The only person he had left was his wife and even she encouraged him to curse God and die because she had already given up on God (**Job 2:9**).

Job's suffering left him broken hearted, weak and weary. He wept and asked God a lot of questions but the one thing He did not do was turn his back away from God. Job had a lot on his plate and instead of trying to deal with it on his own, he took it back to God. **Matthew 11:28-30** encourages us to cast our burdens on God because He cares for us.

Our idea of God up in heaven may lead us to think that He is so far away but He is actually a lot closer to us than we think. He is close to our broken hearts. He does not want us to carry our burdens on our own. In fact, He does not want us to carry any burdens at all. That is why we are encouraged in **1 Peter 5:7** to cast **ALL** our burdens on Jesus so He can give us rest. He sees our broken hearts and He is ready to bind our wounds and heal us (**Psalm 147:3**).

Outpourings Of A Beloved Heart

He knows just where you are hurting right now and He can give you the strength when your heart fails. He can bring you back up again when you seem to be losing hope (**Psalm 73:26**). Please hold on to His word. Hold on to His promises for you today. Remember that even when you think He is far away, He is always near to your broken heart. He loves you.

Prayer: *Dear Heavenly Father, thank You that when my heart is broken, You are near. I pray Lord that when life becomes overwhelming, I will not run away from You. Please help me to always remember that You are closer than I think. In Jesus' name. Amen.*

Today's Affirmation: *I will lay my burdens at His feet and He will heal my broken heart.*

Day 22: Trusting You

Outpourings Of A Beloved Heart

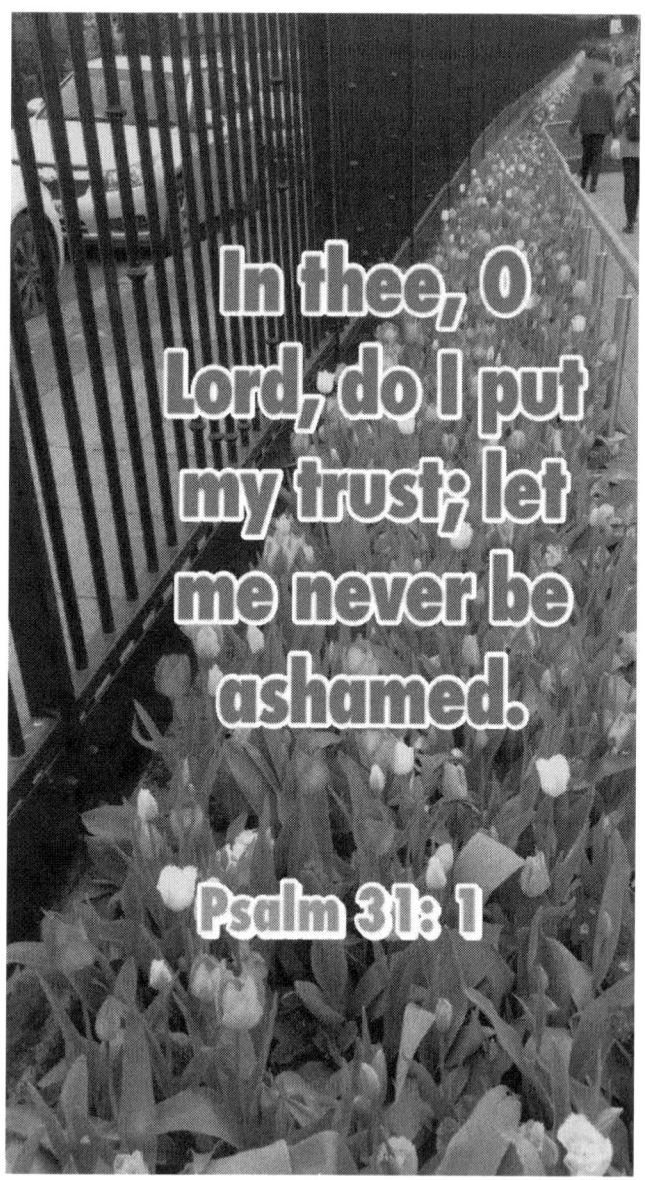

It is hard to trust You.

To take that first step,

When I can't see the staircase.

To walk through the dark tunnel,

When I can't see the light.

It is hard to trust You.

To step into the unknown,

With no idea of what lies ahead.

To get out of the boat,

And walk on the water with You.

It is hard to trust You.

But You make a way for me,

Even in the darkness, You make a way.

You direct my every step,

Till I get to the place You have prepared.

You alone know where I am going,

For You have set this path for me.

What then can I do but trust the omniscient?

Outpourings Of A Beloved Heart

The One who knows all the stars of the universe by name.

The One and only God who knows me by name.

It is hard to trust You,

But say the word Lord and I will follow.

It is hard to trust You,

But I shall do it anyway,

Because trusting You is worth it.

Reflections:

Scripture: Matthew 14:22-33

One of the things we can draw from this Bible passage is that in the midst of trials, we need to fix our eyes on Jesus. When Peter fixed his eyes on Jesus, he was able to walk on the lake. However, when he took his eyes off Jesus and focused on the waves around him, fear set in and his doubts caused him to start sinking. **Focusing on the problem and not the problem solver will not lead you to your destination.**

Another important lesson we can draw from this passage is that in the midst of trials, we need to trust Jesus. **Peter was not the only disciple in the boat that day but he was the only one who trusted Jesus enough to get out of the boat in the first place.** Who are you in this story? When trials come, do you trust Jesus enough to get out of your comfort zone and walk on the water with Him? Or are you like the other disciples who were sitting in the boat and watching the astonishing things happening from afar?

The Bible teaches us that though the oceans roar and the mountains tremble and even though the earth may give way, the Lord Almighty is with us and He is our fortress (**Psalm 34**). **So if the Lord of Hosts is calling you out today to walk on the water with Him, will you trust Him enough to do it?**

It may be hard to trust God through difficult times but it is very worth it. Think about His faithfulness towards you as His beloved one. **He will never withhold anything good from those who walk uprightly (Psalm 84:11).** So as you step out today, be encouraged to put your trust in the Lord of Hosts. **Be like Peter and walk on the water with Jesus.** He will bring you to your expected end. He loves you.

Prayer: *Heavenly Father, thank You because I know You are my refuge and my fortress. You are my God in whom I can put my trust. Teach me Lord today to be like Peter and not be afraid to walk on the water with You. In Jesus' name. Amen.*

Today's Affirmation: *Though I walk through valleys low, my heart will trust in You.*

Day 23: My Hope

Outpourings Of A Beloved Heart

Outpourings Of A Beloved Heart

I dare not hope in my flesh

For it only cares about its own desires

It was made to rebel against my Maker

And rebellious it always will be

I dare not hope in my strength

For I cannot hope in what I do not have

My strength comes from You alone

And without You I am powerless

I dare not hope in my insecurities

For they are nothing but lies

Trying to lure me away from the truth

The truth about my identity in You- as Royalty

I shall only hope in the King of Kings

My Lord and Saviour- Jesus Christ

He has brought me into His light

And He has anchored me safely by His side

Never shall I fear the arrows by day

Neither shall I fear the terrors of the night

I have a hope that is safe and sure

And that hope is in You alone

Reflections:

Scripture: Psalm 62:1-8

Putting our hope in God means we have confidence that something good will happen in the future. When we face challenges, we may put our hope in things that do not last and we can seek truth, love, satisfaction and fulfilment everywhere except from the One who can provide all of these. **The truth remains that our hope lies in Christ alone.**

If we put our hope in anything else other than Christ, whether it be relationships, family, friends, or our abilities, we will end up getting disappointed. **There is nothing else that can substitute the hope we have in Christ.** In **Psalm 62**, we see that King David had difficulties too but he was confident in the God he served. God is the mighty rock on which we can lean on and the only One capable of holding us up in the storm.

Putting your hope in God will make you like the wise man in **Matthew 7:24-27** who built his house on solid rock instead of sand. The Bible says that when the rains came and winds blew against it from all sides, the house stood because its foundation was on the solid rock. **Jesus is the solid rock so stick with Jesus.** He is the reason you can wake up every morning and smile in the midst of trials. He is the reason you

Outpourings Of A Beloved Heart

can keep trying against all odds and He is our only hope in a world that seems hopeless.

It is important to constantly preach hope to yourself because if you don't, you will give way to a discouraged and weary heart. In **Psalm 43:5**, the psalmist cried out **"Why my soul are you downcast? Why so disturbed within me? Put your hope in God, for I will yet praise Him, my Saviour and my God."** In the same way, be encouraged to keep preaching hope to yourself no matter what you are facing today.

As you step out, please do not be disheartened but ask God to fill you with hope today. Things may not look great right now, but as long as you hold on to Jesus, you have a reason to keep pushing forward. Hope in God and you will never be put to shame (**Psalm 25:3**). His unfailing love is still present through trials. He will be your strength and He will be your light. He loves you.

Prayer: *Heavenly Father, thank You for Your words of comfort today reminding me that You alone are my hope. I pray Lord according to Your Word in Romans 15:13 that You fill me with hope and confidence in You. In Jesus' name. Amen*

Today's Affirmation: *I will put my hope in God alone. He will come through for me.*

Day 24: I Will Wait On You

Outpourings Of A Beloved Heart

Outpourings Of A Beloved Heart

Take my weaknesses

Give me Your strength

I will stay here stronger than ever

I will stay here and wait on You

Take my doubts

Give me faith like no other

I will stay here and trust Your good intentions

I will stay here and wait on You

Take my fears

Give me confidence that comes from You

For though fears may come to stifle me

I will stay right here and wait on You

Take every part of me

Give me Your good and perfect will

I won't leave, I won't give up

I will be right here in Your presence and I will be waiting on You

Reflections:

Scripture: Isaiah 40: 28-31

One thing I have noticed about London commuters is that we tend not to be very patient in busy situations. Most people would prefer to be cramped up into a small space on the tube and leave at that very moment than wait a few more minutes for the next tube which will more likely be less packed. To be fair, waiting can be very frustrating sometimes especially when we just want to get things done and get moving.

In our Christian walk, waiting on God can also be something we struggle with especially when we find ourselves in situations where we think we need answers immediately. The waiting season can bring with it discouragement and when we get discouraged we can lose our trust in God. **We often forget that God is working all the time.**

When God promised to make Abraham a great nation, he was 75 years old (**Genesis 12:2-3**) and when his son, Isaac was finally born to him, Abraham was 100 years old (**Genesis 21:5**). It took 25 years from the time God made this promise to when it actually came to pass. Abraham probably got frustrated at some point in his journey. Perhaps he doubted a little bit or perhaps he even found himself at the edge of giving up but he waited on God and he was patient.

In the same way, when God sent Moses to deliver the children of Israel from slavery in Egypt, they did not realise that it was going to take a long time from when the promise was made to when they actually left Egypt. God was working on that promise and He was putting everything together for that promise to eventually happen.

Outpourings Of A Beloved Heart

The Israelites however, wanted immediate relief and a lot of them gave up when the promise was delayed. Discouragement caused them to reject the comforting words Moses gave them from God (**Exodus 6:9-12**) but through it all, God was working to fulfil that promise. **God works for those who wait on Him.**

When God makes a promise to you, He always comes through at the right time. When you wait on God, you do not wait in vain because God has promised to give you strength in the process. Our Bible passage in **Isaiah 40:28-31** says that those who wait on the Lord will never grow tired because He is our continuous source of support to keep us going. It may seem like God is taking a really long time, but He is the only One who knows the perfect time to act. His timing for you is the best there ever could be so please do not grow tired of waiting on Him.

As you step out today, remember that God is working for you as you wait on Him. Be encouraged in Him. Be reminded of how He came through for Abraham and the children of Israel. He will come through for you too. He loves you.

Prayer: *Heavenly Father, thank You so much for reminding me today that You are working for me even as I wait on You. Help me Lord to trust Your good and perfect timing for me and to know that You are faithful and will always fulfil Your promises to me. In Jesus' name. Amen.*

Today's Affirmation: *I will wait patiently for the Lord to act. He is working for me.*

Day 25: To The One Who Holds My Tomorrow

Outpourings Of A Beloved Heart

Outpourings Of A Beloved Heart

To the One who holds my tomorrow,

Sometimes I get scared,

And I think I am not prepared

To encounter the plans You have not shared.

To the One who holds my tomorrow,

Sometimes I just want to know

About all my future highs and lows

And whether I will recede or grow.

To the One who holds my tomorrow,

Do I get that dream job or not?

Do I get that dream man or not?

Do I become that strong independent woman or not?

To the One who holds my tomorrow,

With each passing day, I ask more questions.

The thought of not knowing has led to frustrations,

But one thing I can rely on is Your affection.

To the One who holds my tomorrow,

I may not know what You have planned,

But these things are not for me to understand.

I can trust You because I know that You hold my hand.

Reflections

Scripture: Matthew 6:25-34

I often find myself worrying about what my future will be like and I get anxious when I think about all the uncertainties that lie ahead and all the answers I don't have. I also think about where God is taking me, what His plan is for me, what career choices I am going to make and if I will make the right life decisions. I sometimes wish I could be able to read God's mind or just get a glimpse of what my future would look like so I can better prepare for it. I have learnt however, that **sometimes I will have absolutely no clue where God is taking me and that is okay.**

We are often scared of the unknown and we think if we knew what was going to happen, we will be able to prepare for it. God chooses to reveal what He pleases but even if He doesn't reveal His plans, we can use that as an opportunity to exercise patience and joy in the waiting. **Our human minds will never be able to match His but the one thing we can be sure of is that God is in the future and that is enough**.

Sooner or later everything will begin to make sense so when we totally rely on Him and the guidance of the Holy Spirit, we will never miss the amazing plan He has for us. While it can be scary walking into the unknown with no idea of what lies ahead, we have learnt so far that when we put our hope and trust in God, He will put His peace in our hearts so we do not have to worry about tomorrow.

As you step out today, decide in your heart not to worry about the cares of life such as when you will get married, how many children you will have or where you will end up after university/college. Instead, lay all those worries down at the altar and pray for the guidance of the Holy Spirit to teach you which way to go.

The path may seem scary but God has promised to be with us even when we walk through the valley of the shadow of death. Remember that He is holding your hand as you step into the future and He will make a way for you. He is guiding you along the best possible pathway for your life. He loves you.

Prayer: *Heavenly Father, thank You for reminding me today that You are already in my future. Please help me to trust that You hold my hand and I do not have any reason to be anxious. In Jesus' name. Amen.*

Today's Affirmation: *I know who holds tomorrow and I know He holds my hand.*

Day 26: Give Me Faith

Outpourings Of A Beloved Heart

There's so much going on in my head,

And sometimes I try to do it all on my own.

But what can I do without You Lord?

Please give me faith to trust You.

I wanted to give up and go back.

I thought I was better off back there.

But what exactly is there to go back to?

Please give me faith to trust You Lord.

The pain and hurt come and go,

And I wonder when or if it will ever end.

Why do I ever think about letting go of You?

Please give me faith to trust You Lord.

My heart has gone weary,

And every second crushes me more.

But if I leave You, what will I have left?

Please give me faith to trust You Lord.

I do not know what lies ahead of me,

Outpourings Of A Beloved Heart

And I do not know what the future holds for me,

But I want to face it holding on to You alone

So please give me faith to trust You Lord.

Reflections:

Scripture: Hebrews 11:1-12

The Bible defines faith in **Hebrews 11:1** as the confident assurance that what we hope for will come to pass and it is the evidence of the things we cannot see. So far in this book we have been talking about trusting God, waiting on Him, surrendering all to Him, believing in our identity and worth in Him and also believing that He loves us. Without faith, we will not be able to believe all these things and without faith, we will not be able to please God (**Hebrews 11:6).**

The whole foundation of our relationship with God is based on faith because we do not physically see Him but we can love Him and believe in Him. We do not see Him but we believe that we have been saved by grace through what Christ did for us on the cross. The faith we have in Jesus gives us confidence that if we fix our eyes on Him, we will not lose the race. If we keep looking at the things we can see, we will not be able to focus on God. Faith is all about the things we cannot see. **If we already had what we hoped for, then there will be no reason to hope at all (Romans 8:24-25)**.

Abraham was a man of great faith and we can see evidence of that from the way he lived his life. **Hebrews 11:8** tells us that when God called Abraham to leave his home, Abraham had no idea where he was going but he obeyed because he had faith in God. It was also by faith that Abraham held on to God's promises of making him the father of many nations even though he was far gone in age and so was his wife- Sarah. Abraham was confident in the faithfulness of the One who had made these promises to him.

Where are you in your faith journey?

Are you getting distracted by the things you can see?

Or are you focusing on the hope you cannot see?

Remember as you step out today that Christ is the author and finisher of your faith so if you keep looking at Him, you will not lose sight of what matters. He will give you the confident assurance you need as you walk this Christian journey. He loves you.

Prayer: *Dear Heavenly Father, thank You for all that You are and all You have done for me through Your Son. Please give me faith so I will not be distracted by the things I can see but to fix my eyes on You. In Jesus' name. Amen.*

Today's Affirmation: *I will put my faith in God and fix my eyes on the hope I cannot see.*

Day 27: If Not, You Are Still Good

Outpourings Of A Beloved Heart

When the sun rises each morning,
You are good.
And You watch over me when it sets at night,
For You are still good.

When the flowers burst forth with colour,
You are good.
When the rains come down like showers of blessings,
You are still good.

When my heart is troubled, You give me peace,
For You are good.
And when my heart is grieving Lord, You comfort me
For You are still good.

When the sun shines and brings smiles with it,
You are good.
When layers of snow cover the ground Lord,
You are still good.

In sickness and in health,

Outpourings Of A Beloved Heart

You are good

In the mountain and in the valley Lord,

You are still good.

Your creation and the works of Your hands are good

Your thoughts towards me have always been good

Your plan for me is filled with hope and it is good

Your very nature Lord is good

So then my soul,

Taste and see that the Lord is good.

Run to Him in the day of trouble,

He will deliver you from the hand of your adversary.

But even if He doesn't, He will give you strength to endure,

For He is still good.

Reflections:

Scripture: Daniel 3:8-18

Our Bible passage talks about the story of Shadrach, Meshach and Abednego- the three Hebrew boys well known for refusing to bow down to King Nebuchadnezzar's image of gold. We see in this story that even when they knew about the possibility of being thrown into the burning furnace, they stood their ground and refused to give in. Their reply to the king is what gets me every time I read this story.

First of all, they acknowledged the fact that God is mighty and strong and capable of delivering them from the burning furnace. They knew God was so much greater than King Nebuchadnezzar and that they were standing on the side of victory. But the lesson I would like us to pick up from this story is what they went on to say after that.

Verse 18 says **"But even if He does not, we want you to know, your majesty that we will not serve your god or worship the image of gold you have set up."** These men were confident that even if God did not deliver them out of the burning furnace, they still were not going to bow down.

Can you take some time to think about how powerful such a declaration is? Can you see that in this situation, these men were solely focusing on the goodness of God even though they were about to die? Can you also see from this story that these men clearly knew the type of God they were serving and were confident in His character as a good God?

Another example to illustrate this is from the story of Job. After his wife advised him to curse God and die, Job responded to her in **Job 2:10. "But he said to her, "You speak** as one of the foolish women speaks. Shall we indeed accept good from God and not accept adversity?"** Job also made another powerful declaration to his friends when they came to visit him later on. From **Job 13:15**, he said **"Though He slay me, I will hope in Him."** In other words, Job was saying it did not matter what situation he was in. It did not matter if he was facing triumph or tragedy. He was going to keep hoping in God.

He was solely going to focus on God's goodness. Praises were never going to cease from his mouth. Again, Job was only able to make such a declaration because he was confident in God's character. We see that the faith of these people never wavered because they trusted in God's goodness.

Have you been put in a situation that made you question God's goodness? Sometimes, it may feel like that situation is winning but maybe you are looking at it from the wrong perspective. Please take comfort in what God is telling you today. **The circumstances you are facing do not change who God is.** They will never change what Jesus did for you on the cross and they will not take away your identity in Christ.

Most importantly, **the troubles you are facing will not change the fact that God loves you.** Jesus died to give you victory over every situation. So even though it may seem like your strength is gone and that the trials are winning, remember that Jesus already gave you victory when He died on the cross to give you eternal life. God has always been good and He will remain good. He loves you.

Prayer:

Dear Heavenly Father, thank You for Your words of encouragement that have reminded me about Your good

Outpourings Of A Beloved Heart

nature. Please teach me to say "It is well with my soul" no matter what the situation is. Help me Lord to always see Your goodness and to trust that Your love is present in both triumph and tragedy. In Jesus' name. Amen.

Today's affirmation: *In triumph or in tragedy, God is good. God is good, all the time.*

Questions to think about

> - What have you learnt about how God demonstrates His love for us in trials, suffering and tragedy?

....
....
....
....
....
....
....
....
....
....
....
....
....
....
....
....
....
....
....

PART SEVEN:
OUR FUTURE GLORY

"Yet what we suffer now is nothing compared to the glory He will reveal to us later"

Romans 8:18

Day 28: This Too Shall Pass

Outpourings Of A Beloved Heart

Just like the morning turns into night

Just like it rains and then shines

Just like the rivers flood and then dry up

This too shall pass

Just like the flowers bloom and then wither

Just like wounds bleed and then heal

Just like the rain stops and the rainbow comes

This too shall pass

Just like the dust rises and disappears in the sky

Just like the night soon turns into morning

Just like we can be here today and be gone tomorrow

This too shall pass

Outpourings Of A Beloved Heart

Reflections:

Scripture: 1 Peter 5:6-10

I watched a Christmas movie about a little boy who had just been adopted into a wonderful family and his new parents loved him very much. At the beginning, everything was going so well for this little boy until tragedy struck. His mother was involved in an accident and unfortunately, she died.

I remember during the funeral scene, the priest said something really encouraging to everyone who was there in an attempt to comfort them. He said that even though they were greatly burdened with sorrow, his prayer was that God teaches them to remember that even the pain will pass.

We see in our Bible passage that the Apostle Peter was writing to the elders and the young people in the church to encourage them as they were persecuted for Christ's sake. He encouraged them to stand firm in their faith and to always be alert and sober to resist the devil who is always looking for whom to devour (**Verse 8**).

He also reminded them that all the family of believers around the world were undergoing the same kind of sufferings they were going through (**Verse 9**). They were not alone in their sufferings but those sufferings were only going to be for a little while (**Verse 10**).

Psalm 30:5 reminds us that weeping may endure for a night, but there is joy in the morning. God will restore and strengthen us. It is reassuring to know that God is with us through our trials but it is even more comforting to know that one day, all of this will pass. "A little while" could mean days, months, years or even a lifetime here on earth but no matter how long it takes, it will pass. If your trials make your life seem dark as night, please take heart today. God has promised that they are only going to be for a little while. They will pass.

The night will pass and joy will come in the morning. **God loves you too much to leave you in the dark forever.** Just as the morning brings the sun and with it comes light, Jesus who is the light of the world will drive out all the darkness of the night. He will fill your day with a new hope which only becomes brighter and brighter.

You see all that pain you are feeling in your heart? It will pass.

And also all the worries and anxiety? They will pass.

Even all the fear and terror the night brings? They too will pass.

As you go through today, remember that no matter how bad the situation gets, it too will pass because God loves you.

Prayer: *Dear Heavenly Father, thank You for encouraging my heart today. Thank You for Your promise that the sufferings I go through now will only last a little while. Please teach me to hope in the joy that will come in the morning. In Jesus' name. Amen.*

Today's Affirmation: *Weeping may endure for a night but joy comes in the morning. This too shall pass.*

Day 29: The Streets Of Gold

> He will wipe away every tear from their eyes, and death shall be no more, neither shall there be mourning, nor crying, nor pain anymore, for the former things have passed away
>
> Revelation 21:4

Outpourings Of A Beloved Heart

Tears constantly fall down my cheeks

I feel the pain that shoots through me

My heart breaks from the unending hurt

And my tired, weary soul longs for relief

But take heart oh my soul

Weep no more for there is still hope

There shall be no tears in that city

No tears shall stain those streets of gold

My mouth longs to freely proclaim Your love

I long to say Your name without fear

My heart breaks from the unending persecution

My tired and weary soul longs for freedom

But take heart oh my soul

Fret no more for there is still hope

There shall be no persecution in that city

With freedom you shall walk the streets of gold

All I want to do is serve You

But my flesh is set to rebel against You

The world is filled with temptations and my flesh is weak

My soul longs to love You without restraint

But take heart oh my soul

Do not be discouraged for there is still hope

You shall have transformed bodies in that city

Sin and death shall be no more on the streets of gold

Reflections:

Scripture: Revelation 21:1-4

I watched another Christmas movie about a little boy who found out his mother was dying of cancer during Christmas time. It was going to be her last Christmas and he wanted to do something special for her so he used all the money he had saved to get her a beautiful pair of shoes. This boy knew his mother was going to die but he also knew that she was going to heaven to meet Jesus so he wanted to make sure his mother looked beautiful when she met Jesus in heaven.

Physical death may seem like the end or the final defeat but actually, we can be certain that for God's beloved ones, it is only the beginning of something much greater. Before Jesus resurrected, He had to die first and for us to experience eternal life with Him in heaven, a lot of us will have to die as well. Just like Jesus conquered death and rose up again to sit at the right hand of His Father's throne to worship and glorify

Outpourings Of A Beloved Heart

Him, we too shall be able to rise up on the last day to walk those streets of gold.

This earth is not our home and we are just passing by. It is therefore important to live our lives always focusing on eternity so we will not lose our crown. Jesus said there are many rooms in His Father's house and that the reason He had to go was to prepare a place for us **(John 14:2).** We see in **Revelation 21:4** that in this house, there will be no pain, grief, sorrow, tears, sin, hurt and most of all, no death.

We will have eternal rest in the bosom of our Lord and we will be able to spend eternity worshipping at the Father's throne with the angels. Jesus is coming back for us and when He comes, He will take us out of this world and into the Father's glorious presence. This promise shows that God knows about all our struggles here on earth and great exceeding joy awaits us in heaven. We will have unrestricted access to God's glory.

If we are faithful to the end, we will receive our eternal reward in heaven. All our questions will be answered. Every hidden knowledge will be revealed to us and we will be able to meet Jesus face to face. Thinking about that alone gives my heart great joy and I hope it does that for you too.

As you step out today, remember that physical death is not the end. Jesus is coming soon and He has given you the Holy Spirit to comfort you while you wait for His return. One fact always remains; Jesus loved you yesterday, He loves you today and He will love you forever and always.

Prayer: *Dear Heavenly Father, thank You for the hope I have in You. Thank You because I know that death is not the end. Thank You for Your comforting promises about the* *everlasting joy and glory we will experience with You in heaven. Help me Lord to always hold on to this hope even while here on earth and to fix my eyes on the prize. In Jesus' name. Amen.*

Today's Affirmation: *Jesus will come back to take me home. I will live my life focusing on eternity.*

Day 30: Blessed Be Your Holy Name

Outpourings Of A Beloved Heart

Blessed be Your Holy name

Is all my mouth can ever utter

For You took away my sin and shame

And Your love makes my heart flutter

Blessed be Your Holy name

Is what my soul sings through the pain

For You shared in my sufferings when a man You became

And I'm assured that victory has already been claimed

Blessed be Your Holy name

Will be my song till my last breath

For You have loved me without refrain

Loved me even to the point of death

Blessed be Your Holy name

Shall be my song on the heavenly dance floor

For eternity, Your praises alone shall I proclaim

And praises to You shall it be forevermore

Reflections:

Ephesians 3:20 says "**Now all glory to God, who is able, through His mighty power at work within us, to accomplish infinitely more than we might ask or think**". We have seen so far that God is a loving God, He is mighty, powerful, merciful, and gracious. He is our comforter, our encourager and our peace. He is our deliverer, our Saviour and He is the very definition of love. His abilities are way more than we can ever imagine.

His promises for us are yes and amen. He can change our hearts, renew our minds and He can transform us to be more like Him. He can teach us to love like Him. His love is what changes our hearts and when our hearts have been changed, we can do nothing but bless His name.

When our hearts come to realise just how amazing His love for us is, our mouths can do nothing but sing praises to Him. I do hope that this book has exposed you to the magnificent truths about God's love. I hope that it has encouraged you to see how much God loves you.

I also do hope that you are now able to confidently declare with King David in **Psalm 63:3** that God's love is better than life itself. As you step out today, I pray that your life never stops screaming Jesus and that you never stop telling the whole world about His sovereign love.

Prayer: *Dear Heavenly Father, thank You so much for the love You have for me. Thank You for sending Your Son- Jesus to die so that I may live. Thank You Lord for Your mercies, grace and forgiveness. Thank You for Your comfort, joy and peace. Thank You for Your hand that is upon me and for Your power that is at work in me. I accept Your love today.*

Outpourings Of A Beloved Heart

Please teach me to love like You- selflessly and unconditionally. Teach me Lord to trust Your will for me and to live for You only. Teach me to never stop telling others about You so that I may bring You glory. Help me to always bless Your name in everything I do. In Jesus' name. Amen.

Today's affirmation: *I will bless the Lord at all times. His praise shall continuously be in my mouth.*

Questions to think about

> What have you learnt about God's promise to us of a future glory and what is the hope you have for believing in Jesus Christ?

The End

Acknowledgements

The first time God put this book idea in my heart, it seemed like a joke because writing a book was never part of my plan. This journey has been an amazing one for me because the more I write, the more I believe in the message of the gospel and the more I fall in love with Jesus.

Words can never explain how grateful I am to my Heavenly Father for using me to get these words out there even though I am not worthy. I would be telling a big lie if I said that I did all of this by my own strength. I owe everything to God and it is because of Him that you have this book in your hands so I give Him all the glory.

I strongly believe that credit should be given where it is due and I just want to appreciate my parents Dr Oscar Embola and Mrs Lilian Embola. I can never find the words to describe how much I love them. I am grateful for all the sacrifices they have made for me and my brothers. I am grateful for all their prayers and support throughout my life. God has used them to shape me into the woman I am today and no matter where I go, I will never stop telling the world about the amazing parents I have.

I also want to thank my younger brothers- Prince and Goodridge Embola. I am very fortunate to have gotten the chance to be their elder sister in this world. I know we have fights sometimes and we annoy each other a lot but they have never stopped supporting me. I love them so much and I want to thank them for always being by my side. They have inspired me to grow into the woman God has called me to be.

Outpourings Of A Beloved Heart

I would also like to recognise my spiritual mentor- Minister Michael Okubote and his wife Mrs Tolu Okubote. I am grateful for all the love they've shown me throughout my time at university. I am grateful that they never gave up on me. The love they have shown me has made a great impact in my life and I pray for nothing but favour over their lives.

Finally, I would like to thank my friends- Faith Roman, Francheska Klaud, Tatenda Gochera and Rebecca Anim-Baodu for all their love and support. They believed in me throughout this journey and they always cheered me on. It has been a blessing to have met amazing girls like them and I will never forget all they have done for me.

Also to everyone else who made an impact indirectly to this book, I want to say thank you. All your love and encouragement kept me going. I appreciate you all and I pray God continues to bless and keep you. In Jesus' name. Amen.

Lots of love.

Joanny.

About The Author

Author Joan N. Embola is a Cameroonian/Nigerian girl born and raised in Cameroon. She currently lives in the UK and is studying in London. When not revising or preparing for exams, she loves to write, blog, journal and make videos for her YouTube channel where she encourages others in their Christian journey. She is the founder of **"Love Qualified"** - a ministry dedicated to encouraging others to experience the sovereign love of the one true God who has qualified us to be His beloved ones. She hopes that God uses her work to richly bless and encourage you. You can connect with her on the various platforms below.

Blog: Love Qualified

YouTube channel: Love Qualified

Instagram: @joannywhite

Etsy Shop: Get Inspiration Today

Printed by Amazon Italia Logistica S.r.l.
Torrazza Piemonte (TO), Italy